The Sugar-free Cookbook

Golden Drumsticks (page 66); Swiss Apple Cake (page 107)

The Sugar-free Cookbook

Jennifer Pinker and Veronica Oxley

CHARTWELL
BOOKS, INC.

Food for photography styled by Anne Fayle

We'd like to thank William Brooks in Sydney and Angrev Design in Birkenhead Point, Drummoyne, for supplying the props used in the photographs.

Published by
CHARTWELL BOOKS, INC.
A Division of **BOOK SALES, INC.**
110 Enterprise Avenue
Secaucus, New Jersey 07094

ISBN 0-89009-661-9

Printed and bound in Hong Kong by South China Printing Co.

CONTENTS

ACKNOWLEDGEMENTS

Even a small book has more debts than it can acknowledge. For anything that may be interesting or helpful in these pages we are indebted to our friends and family who have both encouraged and tolerated our numerous experiments. Special thanks to Diane.

FOREWORD

It is often said that diet is the cornerstone of treatment for the diabetic. However, many diabetics find little comfort in this fact. They feel that their daily lives are disrupted by their diet. They feel isolated from their family and friends who can eat at any hour and enjoy whatever foods take their fancy.

When first told about their diabetes and the diet it is natural that many will react with negative thoughts. They think about the foods they are denied rather than the host of foods they can enjoy. They lose their creative urge to try new foods and recipes and instead they plod along eating dull and monotonous meals.

Some go so far as to deny their diabetes because they are embarrassed to admit to friends and colleagues that they need to follow a diet. For such people the authors of this book bring good news. The diabetic diet need not be dull and it can be enjoyed by non-diabetics and diabetics alike.

In fact, the Australian community is being advised to adopt a diet which is close to the diabetic diet. We are being advised as a nation to avoid being overweight, to eat less sugar and less fat, to reduce our alcohol intake and to eat more foods containing starch and fibre. We are even being advised to eat three regular meals each day, no more skipping breakfast or lunch.

This advice is coming from no less an authority than the Commonwealth Department of Health.

No longer apologise for your diet, try new foods and recipes, invite friends to share your meals. Talk to them about cooking with less fat and sugar and share with them some of the exciting recipes for vegetables, salads and fruits which you will find in the pages that follow. You will soon begin to experience some of the enthusiasm for food which is obviously shared by the authors. Meals should be enjoyable as well as nutritious and this book will assist both diabetics and non-diabetics in planning such meals.

Josephine F. Rogers A.M., B.Sc., A.I.D.

We wish to acknowledge the following sources for the carbohydrate count in this book:
Tables of Composition of Australian Foods, by Sucy Thomas and Margaret Corden, Commonwealth Department of Health.
Food Values of Portions Commonly Used, by Charles Church and Helen Church, twelfth edition.
Nutritive Value of American Foods in Common Units, by Catherine F. Adams, United States Department of Agriculture.

PREFACE

This cookbook leads into exciting avenues for experimenting with food. It caters for people who wish to control the calorie and carbohydrate content of their diet, and useful tables accompany each recipe showing the amount of carbohydrate, calories and kilojoules one serve will contain. Especially it is intended that diabetics can know the pleasure of eating without the guilt of breaking their diet. *The Sugar-Free Cookbook* dispenses with the myth that food must be sweetened with sugar to be enjoyed by your family.

Whether you are simply interested in your health or are in fact a diabetic, you can benefit from eliminating refined sugars from your diet. We show how to use your ingenuity by adding dried fruits, fruit juice, citrus rind and sweet spices like cinnamon to naturally sweeten the sauces, cakes, biscuits and desserts. Only occasionally need you add very small quantities of artificial sweeteners to make each recipe taste just right.

We share with you some of our favourite dishes, including useful, basic recipes that form the foundation for the more exotic fare. The emphasis in these dishes is on nutrition, and we show that anyone can enjoy and benefit from a meal that contains less fat and more fibre (from fruit, vegetables and cereals).

Our book removes the mysteries and confusion surrounding diabetic diets and presents a simple and sensible way of eating. At the same time we have added enjoyment, flexibility and convenience to this type of diet. Within the first pages we have explained the principles of diabetic diets, hoping this will be easily understood and trusting you realise the importance of consulting a dietitian for individual advice.

When entertaining, as a diabetic you will feel relaxed in the knowledge that you can share all the meal, including the sweets, and need never again feel 'different' from your guests. Entertaining for both diabetics and diet-conscious people will be easy and assured of success, for the recipes in this cookbook are always delicious and promote health.

A votre santé!

Please refer to sugar substitution chart on page 15
before trying any recipes which require artificial sweeteners.

THE DIABETIC DIET

Back in the bad old days in 1922 when insulin was first discovered, diabetic diets were strict, low carbohydrate regimes, stereotyped and dull! There's no law decreeing that this diet must be boring and unsavoury. The diabetic diet is actually the original natural food diet, with an emphasis on balance: balancing energy intake with insulin, and balancing nutrients with body needs.

Food, like the world, is made of many interrelated parts and until these are broken into smaller units, understanding their function is not easy. Food may be broken up into the largest components: proteins, fats and carbohydrates. These three elements play an important role in your diet. Most foods are a combination of at least two of these components, usually with one predominating. Cane sugar is pure carbohydrate. Cooking oil is pure fat. However, there are no commonly used foods that are pure protein — ricotta cheese and egg whites are significant sources of protein but they also contain water.

Protein foods aid in the repair and maintenance of our body tissues. Meat, fish, poultry, eggs and cheese are particularly rich sources of protein.

Fats are the most concentrated source of energy. Foods that are very high in fat are cream, butter, margarine, sour cream and oil. Fat is the main form in which animals (and human beings) store extra energy, or calories.

Carbohydrates will affect your blood glucose level. When carbohydrates are eaten and digested, they are broken down to form a simple sugar called glucose, which travels in the blood and enters the cells of the body.

We have divided the many carbohydrates into two logical and descriptive groups: simple carbohydrates (sugars), and complex carbohydrates (starches).

1. Simple suggests something that is pure, single or in its basic form. Simple carbohydrates include sugar, glucose, lactose and honey. Little effort is required for our bodies to digest and convert these carbohydrates into glucose. Foods containing these simple carbohydrates cause your blood glucose to rise quite quickly. Avoid eating this type of carbohydrate except when having a 'hypo' (hypoglycaemic attack).

2. Complex — just think of a shopping complex, with a large number of stores under the one roof, so they appear as one store. Complex carbohydrates are a network of several different sugars all bonded together (and include foods such as bread, cereals, fruit, vegetables and milk).

The bonds holding these sugars together do not break easily and it takes the body far longer to convert complex carbohydrates into glucose. Thus it takes far longer for your blood glucose level to rise after a meal. What difference does this make?

Recent research has shown that large swings in blood glucose levels and consistently high blood glucose levels play an active part in the appearance of complications in diabetics.

But balanced diets that are rich in complex carbohydrates and fibre do not produce these large swings in blood glucose levels.

Calories and Kilojoules

The technical term, calories and kilojoules, can be confusing when used by professionals, but it is possible to simplify and explain their meaning.

Calories and kilojoules are the terms used to measure the energy content of food.
Calories are the imperial units of energy.
Kilojoules are the metric units of energy.
1 calorie = 4.2 kilojoules

The energy content of our diets is provided by fats, proteins and carbohydrates. Your blood glucose level is not affected by either fats or proteins, although these will affect your weight if their daily consumption is increased. This means your insulin requirements will increase, as there is more of you to be catered for. The way to rectify such an occurrence is to use the lower kilojoule protein foods like cottage cheese or fish, and keep fats at a minimum.

Milk is a 'complete food' as it contains protein, fat and carbohydrate. It is classified as a carbohydrate because it contains a significant amount of lactose ('sugar of milk').

The Portion System

The carbohydrate count given with each recipe in this book will enable you to control your daily diet with great facility. This will be done under the *portion* system.

As metres are the units used to measure distance, *portions* are the units that measure the carbohydrate content of your foods. There are two *portion* systems operating in Australia:

In New South Wales, one *portion* contains 15 grams of carbohydrate.

In other States, one *portion* contains 10 grams of carbohydrate.

Diabetic *portions* are not necessarily the same size to look at, although they always contain the same amount of carbohydrate. All *portions* are interchangeable, as the diagram shows, so that for example you may substitute cereal for your toast for breakfast. However, when you study carbohydrates a little more, you will find that fruit and vegetable *portions*, and bread and cereal *portions* do affect your blood glucose levels a little differently. Grain-based products have more staying power and will keep your blood glucose level elevated a little longer than fruit and vegetables. This is important to remember at suppertime when it will be some time before you eat again.

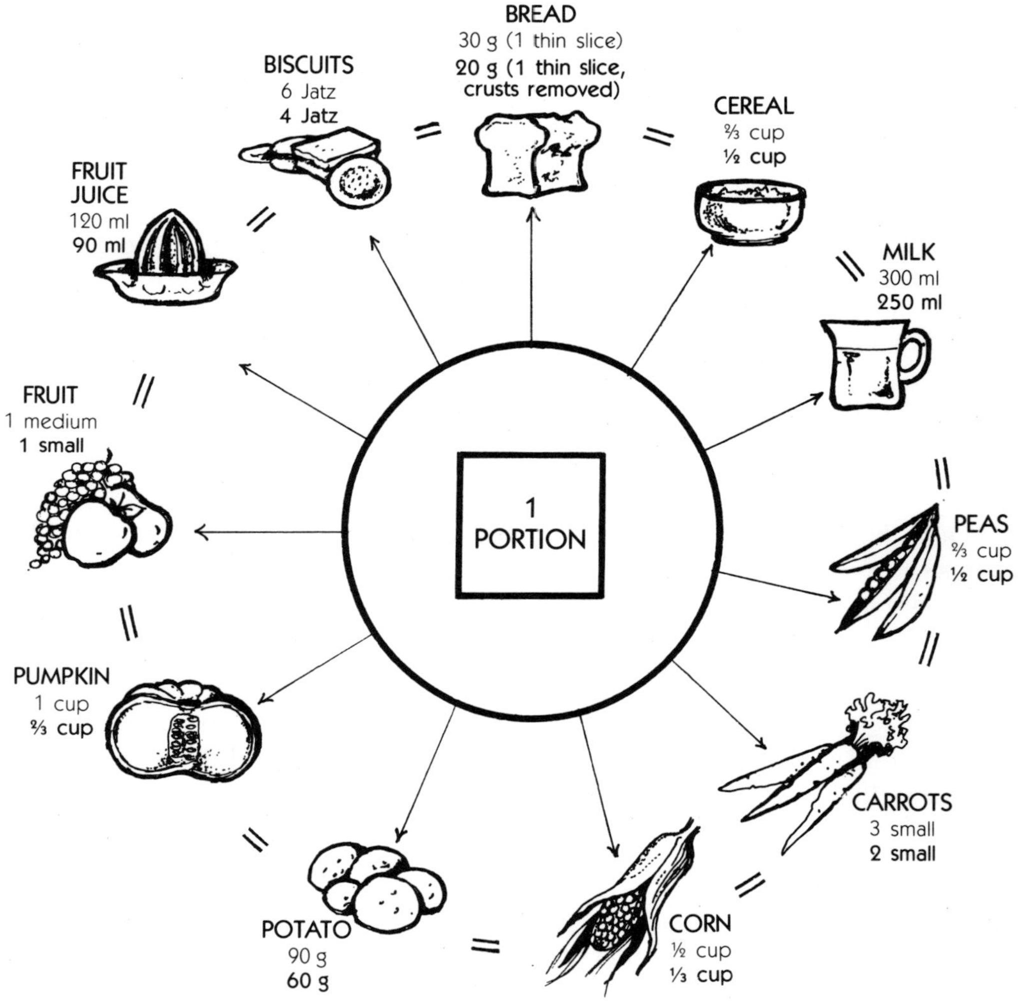

Key

One Portion is equivalent to
15 g carbohydrate (N.S.W.)
10 g carbohydrate (other States)

Meal Planning

How can you fit recipes from a glossy cookbook into your diet? With *The Sugar-free Cookbook*, the grams of carbohydrate are shown per serve, for each recipe. Once a dietitian has told you the number of *portions* you are allowed for each meal, you simply calculate according to your State, the number of *portions* in a serve.

How many *portions* are contained in a serve? Since 15 grams of carbohydrate make one *portion* in New South Wales, you should divide the number of grams of carbohydrate (per serve) by 15. For example, Creamed Rice (see page 97) contains 30 grams of carbohydrate per serve, therefore this allows two *portions* per serve.

In other States, 10 grams of carbohydrate make one *portion*, so Creamed Rice, containing 30 grams of carbohydrate, yields three *portions* per serve.

The majority of your *portions* should come from your main course. It is then necessary to allocate the remainder of your *portions*.

Imagine you are having guests to dinner and you are allowed 45 grams of carbohydrate for your meal (equalling three *portions* in N.S.W. or 4½ *portions* in other States). You may plan your meal as follows:

		g of carbohydrate
First course	**Salmon Mousse (page 39)**	**1**
Main course	**Coq au Vin (page 67)**	**10**
	Anna Potatoes (page 47)	**17**
	Tossed green salad or 'free' vegetables	**0**
Dessert	**Apple Crumble (page 104)**	**16**
		44

This is sufficiently close to the sample meal (45 g of carbohydrate). The majority of the carbohydrate derives from the main course and dessert. However, in the following menu the carbohydrate derives mostly from the first and main courses:

		g of carbohydrate
First course	**Old-fashioned Tomato Soup (page 28)**	**14**
Main course	**Coq au Vin (page 67)**	**10**
	Anna Potatoes (page 47)	**17**
	Tossed green salad or 'free' vegetables	**0**
Dessert	**Strawberry Soufflé (page 103)**	**4**
		45

Are Six Meals a Day Necessary? With the exception of some diabetics on tablets and those being treated by diet alone, you should have snacks between three main meals every day. Eating regularly allows your carbohydrate intake to be spaced over the whole day which complements the action of insulin.

Insulin is the substance that allows your body to keep your blood glucose level within the normal limits. Once you have had your injection, the insulin begins to work and your blood glucose level begins to fall. The importance of your meals is in preventing your blood glucose from falling too low. Thus eating three meals and three snacks is the best way to prevent this from happening. You should never miss supper, as there are many hours to pass before breakfast time.

How does Fibre help? Fibre helps to support and protect plants. It is present in the fibrous tissue of fruit and vegetables, the outer layer of cereal grains and in the skins of fruit and vegetables. Fibre needs a lot of chewing and cannot be digested by humans. It acts like a fishing net, trapping the carbohydrate and forcing the body to take longer to convert the carbohydrate into the simple form of glucose. This delay in the rate of conversion is very important because it helps prevent the high swings in blood glucose levels following a meal.

To a certain degree, fibre will also act as a natural appetite-control mechanism, the extra bulk making you feel satiated sooner.

Do you automatically think of unprocessed bran when we say 'fibre'? All wholegrain flours and products, fruit and vegetables and their skins, seeds and nuts contain fibre. Experiment with wholemeal flour instead of white in your recipes.

Products Suitable for the Diabetic

The journal *Diabetes Care* said in 1980:

> The use of glucose and glucose-containing simple sugars has been discouraged in the diets of most diabetic patients in an attempt to prevent rapid rises in blood glucose levels . . . The ideal substitute should not raise blood sugar levels significantly and should not have undesirable side-effects.[1]

Some special foods marketed as 'Suitable for Diabetics' contain appreciable simple sugars and kilojoules, the amounts of which may not be stated. It is important to realise this.

The sweeteners commonly used by diabetics generally fall into two categories:

a) **Nutritive** sweeteners contain varying amounts of simple sugars or sugar alcohols. These include lactose, fructose, sorbitol, mannitol, xylotol . . . and the products are often labelled 'Carbohydrate Modified'.
b) **Non-nutritive** sweeteners do not contain carbohydrate. Many of the products containing these sweeteners are marketed as Low Joule[2]/Calorie or sugar-free. These include saccharins and cyclamates.

As nutritive sweeteners contain carbohydrates, they must be subtracted from the *portions* in your diet, so they are not recommended. A moderate use of the non-nutritive sweeteners, saccharins and cyclamates, is quite acceptable as replacement for sugar.

As people become more aware of the effects of a high sugar consumption, the number of low joule products is rapidly increasing. Products that are suitable to use at present include:

Low Joule soft drinks, Low Joule cordials, Low Joule toppings, Low Joule dressings, Low Joule pickles, Low Joule fruit juice drinks, Low Joule jams and marmalades (not carbohydrate modified), unsweetened canned fruit, unsweetened fruit juices, liquid and tablet artificial sweeteners.

Using Artificial Sweeteners

Throughout the cookbook we have replaced refined sugars with dried fruits and juices. However, in some of the recipes, particularly cakes and desserts, it was necessary to add minimal amounts of artificial sweetener. Sweeteners are available in liquid, tablet and powdered form. Liquid and tablet sweeteners are suitable for diabetics as they contain no carbohydrate. Powdered sweeteners contain carbohydrates that are unsuitable for the diabetic. No powders have been used in our recipes.

High temperatures and prolonged cooking may alter the composition of the sweetener and produce an unpleasant flavour. Therefore whenever possible add the sweetener after cooking. The amount of sweetener used is of vital importance to the success of the recipe, as a heavy hand will give the finished product a bitter taste. The manufacturer's recommended substitutions of sweetener for sugar is usually a little high. As a guideline, use up to ¼ teaspoon of liquid sweetener per serving, irrespective of the amount of sugar it is replacing. In the recipes we have replaced 1½ tablespoons of sugar with 1 teaspoon of sweetener. You may find you prefer the finished product slightly sweeter than we have stated; if so, add a little more sweetener to those recipes. It is best to choose and stay using a sweetener that suits yourself, and the correct substitution for sugar will become known to you through cooking results.

As all sweeteners vary in concentration, for your convenience we have included the following chart of manufacturers' recommended substitutions. **The amounts stated are equivalent to 1 teaspoon of the liquid artificial sweetener used in our recipes.**

Type	Amount
Liquid	
Hermesetas	**1 teaspoon**
Sucaryl	**1 teaspoon**
Sugarella	**½ teaspoon**
Sugarine	**12 drops**
Sweetex	**6 drops**
Tablets	
Hermesetas	**8**
Saccharin	**4**
Saxin	**8**
Sucaryl	**8**
Sucron	**8**
Sugarella	**8**
Sugarine	**4**
Sweetex	**8**

1. *Diabetes Care*, vol. 3 no. 2, Mar–Apr 1980, pp. 390–392.
2. Kilojoules/Joules are the metric units of energy. The Calorie was the imperial measure.

FREE FOODS

These foods contain either very little or no carbohydrate. (Some are high in energy and need to be limited if trying to reduce weight). A moderate intake will not affect your blood glucose level and can be enjoyed at any meal.

LOW ENERGY

Beverages

beef tea
stock cube in water
coffee
tea
juice of one lemon
tomato juice (one glass)
soda water
mineral water
water
artificially sweetened soft drinks/cordials

Vegetables

asparagus
bean sprouts
broccoli
capsicum
cauliflower
celery
chicory
chillies
chives
choko
cucumber
dill pickles
fennel
garlic
leafy greens
lettuce
marrow
olives
parsley
radish
silverbeet
spinach
beans (small serve)
mushrooms (1–2)
tomato (one)
zucchini (small serve)

Other

essences
vinegar
fish paste
meat paste
gelatine, junket tablets
herbs
spices
mustard
soya sauce
unprocessed bran
vegemite, marmite, promite
Worcestershire sauce
artificially sweetened products (page 14)

MEDIUM ENERGY

Fats

cream
butter
margarine — cooking
table
polyunsaturated
saturated
sour cream
oil — saturated
polyunsaturated
copha
mayonnaise
suet

Proteins

hard cheeses
Parmesan cheese
cream cheese
canned fish in oil
processed meats
beef, lamb
bacon
duck

HIGH ENERGY

Proteins

cottage cheese
ricotta cheese
eggs
chicken and turkey
fresh fish
canned fish in brine
organ meats
rabbit
veal
shellfish

SUGAR-CONTAINING FOODS

These foods contain significant amounts of simple carbohydrate (sugars) and are best avoided except when treating a 'hypo' (hypoglycaemic attack) or undertaking strenuous exercise.

BEVERAGES
cordial
soft drink
fruit juice drinks
tonic water
cider
glucose-enriched drinks
glucose-enriched powdered vitamin supplement
fruit nectars
condensed milks
flavoured yoghurts
milkshakes

BISCUITS AND CAKE
sweet and cream biscuits
cakes
sweet buns
donuts sprinkled with sugar
donuts with jam/icing

OTHER
jams, marmalades
chutney
sweet pickles
candied peel
glacé fruit
diet products not recommended (page 14)

DESSERTS AND PASTRY
sweet desserts
instant puddings
sweet jelly
iceblocks, paddlepops
milk ices
fancy ice creams
canned fruit in syrup
preserved fruit in syrup
sweetened pastry
sweet pies

CEREALS
sweetened muesli
sugar-coated cereals

LOLLIES
health food bars
chocolate/carob bars
candy
sweet popcorn

SUGARS
glucodin
glucose
honey
malt
maple/golden syrup
treacle, molasses
raw, brown, white sugar

BRUNCH

Start each day the proper way, by eating a good breakfast. People who sit down to a good breakfast are noticeably more capable of performing a morning's work efficiently.

Here are some easy-to-prepare, yet healthy breakfast ideas:

unsweetened muesli topped with natural yoghurt
cottage cheese on wholegrain toast
(¼ cup cottage cheese has more protein than 1 egg – and fewer kilojoules)
natural yoghurt and chopped fresh fruit
pour buttermilk over your favourite wholewheat cereal
a poached egg on mixed grain muffins

As eggs and brunch are almost synonymous, it is important to understand cooking with eggs. Are they fresh? When placed in a basin of cold salted water, fresh eggs will sink on their side. If it stands on end, or floats, it is not fresh. Air penetrates the porous shell of stale eggs. They are best stored, point end down, in the body of the refrigerator. If you are an avid egg user, they may be stored in a cool place for a short time only.

Many recipes call for either egg whites or yolks. Egg whites keep well for several weeks if stored in a clean jar in the refrigerator. Try to use the yolks in the next meal by adding to fruit juice, mashed vegetables, pastry, stirred or baked custard or use to bind meatloaves, patties and stuffings.

SPANISH OMELETTE (photograph opposite)

Cook an extra potato or two with your evening meal and try this colourful omelette for brunch.

Serves 2

One serve contains	
Carbohydrate	11 g
Calories	290
Kilojoules	1215

1 slice bacon, trimmed and chopped
1 tablespoon chopped onion
1 small clove garlic, crushed
1 tablespoon chopped green pepper
1 medium cooked potato, diced
1 medium tomato, roughly chopped
3 eggs
⅓ cup (1½ oz) grated Cheddar cheese
¼ teaspoon mixed herbs
½ teaspoon paprika
½ teaspoon salt
freshly ground black pepper

Using an omelette pan, sauté the bacon, onion, green pepper and garlic until the onion is transparent. Add the chopped potato and tomato and cook for a further 3 minutes.

Lightly beat the eggs with the cheese, herbs, paprika, salt and pepper. Pour over the vegetables. Cook over a low heat until the eggs are set. Do not stir.

If necessary, put the omelette under a hot grill until the top is just set. Serve hot, cut into portions.

Spanish Omelette (page 18)

Bouillabaisse (page 29); Pumpkin Cheese Soup (page 31)

20

BASIC OMELETTE

Do not expect your first omelette to be beautiful. But once you have mastered the technique your omelettes will look as good as they taste.

Serves 1

3 eggs
1 tablespoon water
salt and pepper
15 g (½ oz) butter or margarine

Total recipe contains	
Carbohydrate	neg.
Calories	315
Kilojoules	1320

Place omelette pan over low heat to warm slowly. Break eggs into a small mixing bowl, add water, salt and pepper. Beat lightly with a fork until the eggs run smoothly through the prongs of the fork.

Increase the heat of the pan, add the butter. When it starts to sizzle pour in the omelette mixture. Using a fork, stir the mixture in the centre a few times, and bring the eggs from the side of the pan towards the middle, like the spokes of a wheel. This allows uncooked egg to run to the side and set. Continue until the omelette is lightly cooked, the underside light golden brown and the centre creamy.

Lift the edge of the omelette nearest the pan handle, fold over one third and gently shake the omelette towards the edge. To turn out, hold the omelette pan with the left hand underneath the handle, turn over with a quick flick of the wrist and turn out on to a warmed plate, so making another fold. Serve immediately.

Variations

Sprinkle any of the following over the lightly cooked eggs before folding the omelette. Prepare beforehand and keep warm while making omelettes.

Fines Herbes: Chopped parsley, chives and tarragon.
Cottage: Plain, chive or pineapple cottage cheese.
Mushroom: 6–8 sliced mushrooms, lightly sautéed in butter.
Cheese: Grated Cheddar or Swiss cheese.
Ham: Finely chopped cooked ham.
Avocado: Diced avocado, crumbled bacon and cottage cheese.
Tomato and Onion: 1 small chopped tomato and sautéed onion.

COTTAGE SCRAMBLED EGGS

Creamy cottage cheese keeps the eggs moist while adding its own subtle flavour. Chives, bacon or parsley can also be added.

Serves 2

¼ cup (2 oz) cottage cheese
3 eggs
salt and pepper
20 g (⅔ oz) butter

One serve contains	
Carbohydrate	neg.
Calories	190
Kilojoules	795

Place cottage cheese, eggs, salt and pepper in a blender or processor; blend until smooth. Alternatively, push cottage cheese through a sieve and mix in other ingredients.

Melt the butter in a small frying pan over a gentle heat. Pour in egg mixture and, using a broad wooden spatula, move egg slowly across pan as the egg thickens. Continue until the eggs are fully cooked but not dry.

Serve immediately sprinkled with chopped fresh herbs if desired.

PRAWN OMELETTES

Serves 4

One serve contains	
Carbohydrate	9 g
Calories	315
Kilojoules	1320

Sauce:

1 tablespoon cornflour (cornstarch)
1 cup (8 fl oz) strong chicken stock
2 teaspoons soy sauce
few drops liquid artificial sweetener
salt

Omelettes:

8 eggs
250 g (8 oz) cooked shelled prawns (shrimps), roughly chopped
250 g (8 oz) bean sprouts, chopped
60 g (2 oz) fresh mushrooms, finely chopped
1 stick celery, diced
½ cup chopped spring onions (scallions)
1 teaspoon salt
freshly ground black pepper
30 g (1 oz) butter or margarine

Sauce: Blend the cornflour and the stock together in a saucepan. Stir over gentle heat until the sauce boils and thickens. Add soy sauce, sweetener and salt to taste. Cover and keep warm while making omelettes.

Omelettes: Beat the eggs until slightly frothy. Add prawns, vegetables, salt and pepper. Melt half the butter in a large frying pan (just to cover the base). Cook eight small omelettes (four at a time) adding extra butter when necessary. Cook both sides until golden brown and eggs have set. Stack omelettes and keep warm while cooking the remaining omelettes. To serve, spoon the sauce over the omelettes.

COTTAGE CHEESE PANCAKES

Makes 12 pancakes, 10 cm (4 in) in diameter

One pancake contains	
Carbohydrate	4 g
Calories	86
Kilojoules	360

1 cup (8 oz) cottage cheese
½ cup (2 oz) wholemeal flour
2 tablespoons polyunsaturated oil
4 eggs, separated
pinch salt

Preheat a lightly greased frying pan. Place all ingredients except egg whites into a blender, blend until smooth (add a little milk if mixture is too thick to blend). In a large bowl, beat egg whites until stiff then fold in the blended mixture.

Drop by tablespoons on to a heated frying pan. Cook until the underside is golden brown, turn and cook the other side. Keep warm until serving time.

Serve hot, buttered or with your choice of topping, such as reheated casseroles, a savoury cottage cheese mixture, ratatouille or vegetables in a cheese sauce.

Variations

1. Add ½ cup (2 oz) grated Cheddar cheese to the mixture. Serve plain with butter.
2. Add ½ cup (2 oz) chopped ham or bacon to the mixture. Serve plain with butter or topped with creamed corn.
3. Add 1 teaspoon grated orange rind, 1 teaspoon liquid artificial sweetener and ½ teaspoon mixed spice (optional). Serve with cottage cheese or yoghurt and fruit.

SAVOURY ONION SLICE

Serves 6

One serve contains	
Carbohydrate	29 g
Calories	340
Kilojoules	1425

Base

1½ cups (6 oz) wholemeal self-raising flour
½ cup (2 oz) wheatgerm
½ teaspoon salt
30 g (1 oz) butter or margarine, melted
⅔ cup (5½ fl oz) milk (approximately)

Topping

2 teaspoons butter or margarine
1 large onion, thinly sliced
1 slice bacon, trimmed and chopped
1 x 250 g (8 oz) carton light sour cream
2 eggs
salt
freshly ground pepper
½ cup (2 oz) grated Cheddar cheese

Preheat the oven to 190°C (375°F/Gas 5).

Base: Mix the flour, wheatgerm and salt in a medium bowl. Add the melted butter and sufficient milk to form a soft dough. Spread in a greased 20 cm (8 in) square cake tin.

Topping: Sauté the onion in butter until transparent. Spread on base and top with the chopped bacon. Beat the cream and eggs together, season with salt and pepper, pour over bacon. Top with the grated cheese and bake for approximately 30 minutes.

Courtesy of Bread Research Institute of Australia.

COUNTRY MORNING MUESLI

The muesli will keep for weeks in an airtight container. Try our version, then invent your own.

Yields 9 cups

One serve contains	
Carbohydrate	18 g
Calories	239
Kilojoules	1000

Allow ½ cup per serve

4 cups (12 oz) rolled oats
1 cup (5 oz) sunflower seeds
1½ cups (4½ oz) desiccated coconut
½ cup (1½ oz) wheatgerm
1 cup (1 oz) unprocessed bran
1 cup (5 oz) sultanas or raisins

Place the oats and sunflower seeds in a baking dish. Toast in a moderate oven or under a griller for 10 minutes. Add coconut, wheatgerm and bran, cook for a further 10 minutes or until golden. Stir frequently to prevent burning.

Add the sultanas, place in an airtight container and store.

CRAB CROUTONS

Serves 8

One serve contains	
Carbohydrate	14 g
Calories	175
Kilojoules	735

1 large French bread stick
2 x 170 g (5½ oz) cans crab
15 g (½ oz) butter
2 spring onions (scallions), chopped
1 small can champignons (button mushrooms) in brine
4 eggs, separated
1 cup (8 fl oz) milk
2 tablespoons chopped parsley
squeeze lemon juice
salt
freshly ground pepper

Preheat the oven to 190°C (375°F/Gas 5). Cut the French bread in half lengthwise and scoop out the soft middle, leaving a 1 cm (½ in) border. Make breadcrumbs from the soft bread, measure 2 cups of crumbs and place in a large bowl. Add crab.

Sauté the spring onions in the butter. Cool.

Drain and slice the champignons, add to the crab with the spring onions, egg yolks, milk and parsley. Season to taste with lemon juice, salt and pepper. Beat the egg whites until stiff, fold into mixture. Brush the bread stick with melted butter and fill halves with mixture. Place on an oven tray and bake for 15–20 minutes. Cut into 8 serving pieces [approximately 13 cm (5 in) sections]. Serve with a side salad.

Courtesy of Bread Research Institute of Australia.

SAVOURY BREAD BOATS

Most bread rolls are suitable for this recipe, but try to buy fancy shaped rolls to enhance the appearance, because presentation counts!

Serves 4

One serve contains	
Carbohydrate	32 g
Calories	447
Kilojoules	1870

4 horseshoe bread rolls
1 cup (8 oz) drained tuna
1 cup (4 oz) grated Cheddar cheese
1 tablespoon minced onion
1 tablespoon finely chopped celery
¼ cup (1½ oz) chopped unsalted peanuts
½ cup (4 oz) cottage cheese
2 teaspoons lemon juice
dash Tabasco sauce
extra ½ cup (2 oz) grated Cheddar cheese

Preheat the oven to 180°C (350°F/Gas 4). Cut the top off each bread roll, being careful not to take too much of the roll with it. Discard the tops. Scoop out the centres of the rolls and make into breadcrumbs. Mix the crumbs with remaining ingredients except the extra cheese. Place the mixture into the hollowed rolls and top with grated cheese.

Place rolls on a baking sheet and bake for 15–20 minutes or until hot.

SPOON BREAD

This bread is served hot, straight from the oven. Cornmeal is to be found in health food stores.

Serves 4

One serve contains	
Carbohydrate	30 g
Calories	394
Kilojoules	1650

60 g (2 oz) butter or margarine
2½ cups (20 fl oz) milk
1 cup (4 oz) cornmeal
½ cup (2 oz) grated cheese
½ teaspoon marjoram
1 teaspoon salt
4 eggs, separated

Preheat the oven to 190°C (375°F/Gas 5). Combine the butter and 2 cups of the milk in a saucepan. Heat until the butter has melted and the milk boils. Remove from heat and whisk in the cornmeal, cheese, marjoram and salt. Add the remaining milk and beat until smooth, about 1–2 minutes. Beat in egg yolks, one at a time. Whisk egg whites until stiff, lightly fold into batter.

Pour mixture into a lamington tin and bake for 35 minutes or until puffed and brown. Serve immediately with a tossed salad.

Variation

Add 2 slices chopped ham or bacon to the mixture.

BRIMFUL PEPPERS

A perfect slimmer's lunch — satisfying and brimming over with flavour and colour.

Serves 6

One serve contains	
Carbohydrate	7 g
Calories	81
Kilojoules	340

6 small firm red peppers
3 tomatoes, skinned, chopped and drained
¾ cup (6 oz) cottage cheese
150 g (5 oz) tuna in brine, drained
1 tablespoon lemon juice
1 tablespoon chopped parsley
3 tablespoons chopped chives
garlic salt to taste
freshly ground black pepper
6 cup-shaped lettuce leaves for serving

Slice off the tops of the peppers, remove the seeds and white flesh. Blanch in boiling water for 30 seconds.

Combine the chopped tomatoes, cottage cheese, tuna, lemon juice, parsley, chives, garlic salt and pepper in a large bowl. Mix well. Fill the hollowed peppers with this mixture and replace the tops. Arrange the stuffed peppers on the lettuce leaves. Serve chilled.

Variation

Substitute tomatoes for red peppers, but do not blanch tomatoes.

COTTAGE CHEESE LOAF

The final product has a similar texture and taste to a traditional meat loaf.

Serves 3

One serve contains	
Carbohydrate	21 g
Calories	237
Kilojoules	990

1 cup (8 oz) cottage cheese
1 cup (3 oz) rolled oats
1 large egg
1 tablespoon soy sauce
1 teaspoon mixed herbs
few drops liquid artificial sweetener

Preheat the oven to 180°C (350°F/Gas 4). Combine all the ingredients in a bowl. Mix thoroughly. Press mixture into a greased small casserole dish. Bake for 20–30 minutes or until cooked. Serve hot or cold with salad.

HEALTHY LUNCHES

To replace those junky munchies, we recommend more nutritious lunches that will promote good health. For example:

Fresh fruit salad topped with yoghurt.
Pawpaw or rock melon halves filled with ricotta cheese and chopped dates.
Lebanese flatbread spread with tabbouleh, hoummus or falafel.
Taco shells filled with cottage cheese, lettuce, tomato, avocado and taco sauce.
Wheat crackers topped with chicken, sprouts and mayonnaise.
Thick shake blended from yoghurt, banana and nuts.
Jaffles or toasted sandwiches, wholegrain sandwiches and bread rolls with the following selected fillings:

sliced apple with cottage cheese, celery and nuts
avocado, crumbled bacon and sprouts
ricotta cheese, chopped almonds, dried apricots and lemon juice
flaked crab, camembert cheese, chives and paprika
grated carrot, cheese and chopped dates
hard-boiled egg, mashed sardine and onion rings
blue cheese, sliced pear and walnuts
mashed banana, dried fruit and cinnamon
ham, sprouts and cottage cheese with pineapple
ricotta cheese with peanut butter and cucumber

SOUP

Soup making is not at all as difficult or time-consuming as many people seem to imagine. The most wonderful thing about soup is that it practically makes itself. It's just so easy to put the ingredients into a large pot and leave it to simmer all day. Or, if time is short, try a simple speedy soup such as Pumpkin Cheese Soup or Crab Bisque.

Soup can be adapted to the occasion. A small bowl of soup can be a light and delicate start to a meal, or a generous hot mug of soup served with fresh crusty bread is a satisfying meal in itself.

Home-made stock is the basis of all good soups. Stock is usually made from ingredients which would otherwise be discarded or are very cheap to buy. You can never make too much stock because, once made, it can be frozen until needed. Stock cubes can be used, but they are quite salty and lack the characteristic jellied quality of the real bone stock. A well-prepared soup should be free from any greasiness, so use a fat-free stock and skim the soup during cooking.

There are always occasions when we resort to canned soups. Next time try something a little different: buttermilk adds a tang to canned cream soups such as tomato, celery and chicken. It has the goodness of whole milk but only half the kilojoules.

LENTIL AND VEGETABLE SOUP

This hearty soup is a meal in itself served with hot wholemeal bread rolls. The soup can be made the day before, adding the Polish sausage just before serving.

Serves 12

One serve contains	
Carbohydrate	30 g
Calories	320
Kilojoules	1340

2.5 litres (10 cups) cold water
500 g (1 lb) green lentils, soaked overnight and drained
250 g (8 oz) lean bacon pieces, chopped
3 medium carrots, diced
1 leek, trimmed and chopped
1 parsnip, chopped
2 sticks celery, chopped
2½ teaspoons salt
30 g (1 oz) butter or margarine
2 medium onions, finely chopped
2 tablespoons flour
1½ tablespoons white vinegar
250 g (8 oz) Polish sausage (or similar), chopped
thyme
freshly ground black pepper

Bring the water to the boil in a large saucepan. Remove from heat and add the lentils, bacon, carrots, leek, parsnip, celery and salt. Return to heat and allow to simmer for 45–50 minutes. Meanwhile, heat the butter in a heavy-based saucepan. Sauté the onions until soft. Stir in the flour, cook a further 3–4 minutes or until the flour is golden brown but not burnt. Remove from heat, add about 1 cup of the soup, and stir until well-blended. Stir in the vinegar then add the sauce mixture to the soup.

Cover and simmer for another hour or until the lentils are tender (add more water if the soup gets too thick). Add the Polish sausage, thyme and pepper. Simmer for a further 5–10 minutes or until the sausage is heated through. Check seasoning and serve with hot bread rolls or toast.

BEEF STOCK

To remove fat from the stock, chill until the fat sets on the top, then lift off. A well-strained stock yields no carbohydrate or energy.

Yields 8 cups (2 litres)

2 kg (4 lb) meaty soup bones
1 onion, quartered
2 medium carrots, cut into large pieces
1 turnip, quartered
1 stalk celery, cut into sticks
bouquet garni
12 black peppercorns
parsley stalks (optional)
3–4 teaspoons salt

Rinse the bones under cold water. Place in a large saucepan and cover with cold water. Slowly bring to the boil, skimming when necessary. Add remaining ingredients, cover and simmer for 2½–3 hours.

Strain stock through a fine sieve into a large bowl, discard bones and vegetables. Cover and chill. Remove fat. The stock can be stored in the refrigerator or the freezer. Freeze in small containers such as ice cube trays, then transfer to a plastic bag. Add the cubes to casseroles, sauces and gravies.

OLD-FASHIONED TOMATO SOUP

Serves 10

One serve contains	
Carbohydrate	14 g
Calories	96
Kilojoules	400

2 tablespoons oil
4 medium onions, roughly chopped
6 cloves garlic, crushed
2 kg (4 lb) ripe tomatoes, roughly chopped
3 large carrots, sliced
1 stick celery, sliced
2 bay leaves
3 cups (24 fl oz) beef stock
½ teaspoon marjoram
½ teaspoon mixed herbs
1 teaspoon salt
freshly ground black pepper
chopped mint or parsley for garnish

Heat the oil in a large saucepan. Add the onion and garlic and cook until the onion is soft. Add all remaining ingredients and simmer gently for 40–50 minutes. Cool, and purée in a processor or blender.

Reheat and check seasoning before serving. Garnish with chopped parsley or mint and serve with fresh bread rolls or toast.

FISH STOCK

This stock yields no carbohydrate or energy.

Yields 8 cups (2 litres)

2 fish heads
shells from prawns
8 cups (2 litres) water
2 bay leaves
salt
10 peppercorns

Wash fish heads and prawn shells thoroughly. Combine all ingredients in a large saucepan. Bring to the boil; cover and let simmer for 1 hour. Strain. Refrigerate or freeze until needed.

BOUILLABAISSE (photograph on page 20)

A thick fish soup. It is a Mediterranean specialty, with each region having its own recipe. Bouillabaisse can be a main course meal in its own right, or you can serve the broth first, followed by the seafood.

Serves 10

One serve contains	
Carbohydrate	6 g
Calories	263
Kilojoules	1100

1 tablespoon oil
4 medium onions, chopped
8 tomatoes, chopped
8 cups (2 litres) fish stock (see previous recipe)
1 piece orange rind
1 kg (2 lb) white fish fillets, cut into 4 cm (1½ in) pieces (a mixture of gemfish and red fish is good)
500 g (1 lb) green prawns (shrimps), peeled
24 mussels, scrubbed
250 g (8 oz) scallops
generous pinch of saffron
salt
freshly ground pepper
chopped parsley

Heat the oil in a large saucepan. Sauté the onions until soft. Add the tomatoes and cook a further 5 minutes. Pour in the stock and orange rind and bring to the boil.

Sprinkle the seafood with the saffron. Add the fish pieces to the stock and cook briskly for 5 minutes. Season with salt and pepper. Add the remaining seafood and cook for another 3–5 minutes or until the fish is tender and the mussels have opened. Serve in a soup tureen sprinkled with chopped parsley.

CHICKEN STOCK

This stock can be used to prepare soups, sauces, and adds flavour to casseroles. It can be frozen for months or stored in the refrigerator for up to ten days. Chicken stock is free of carbohydrate and energy.

Yields 12 cups (3 litres)

1 x 1.5 kg chicken
2 large onions, roughly chopped
2 carrots, sliced
2 celery stalks, cut into 5 cm (2 in) pieces
2 bay leaves
1 whole clove
1 teaspoon chervil
½ teaspoon thyme
½ teaspoon rosemary
salt
whole peppercorns
12 cups (3 litres) water

Place all ingredients in a large saucepan. Bring to the boil and simmer for 2 hours. Remove the chicken, which can then be used in any recipe calling for cooked chicken, and strain the stock. Allow to cool and skim off the fat.

CRAB BISQUE

A rich, thick, creamy soup with the delicate flavour of crab.

Serves 4

One serve contains	
Carbohydrate	13 g
Calories	345
Kilojoules	1445

45 g (1½ oz) butter
1 small onion, finely chopped
2 tablespoons finely chopped green pepper
3 tablespoons flour
1½ cups (12 fl oz) chicken stock
250 g (8 oz) can crab, flaked
(reserve some for garnish)
1½ cups (12 fl oz) milk
½ cup (4 fl oz) cream
1 tablespoon dry sherry
dash Tabasco sauce
salt
freshly ground pepper
chopped parsley for garnish

Heat the butter in a frying pan. Sauté the onion and green pepper until soft but not brown. Stir in the flour and cook for another minute (do not allow the flour to brown).

Remove from heat and gradually add the chicken stock. Return to heat and stir until the sauce boils. Simmer for 5 minutes. Add the crab, milk, cream, sherry and Tabasco sauce. Season to taste with salt and pepper.

Gently re-heat and serve garnished with the reserved crab meat and chopped parsley.

CHILLED CUCUMBER SOUP

This soup can also be served hot with fresh crusty bread.

Serves 10

One serve contains	
Carbohydrate	5 g
Calories	99
Kilojoules	415

2 medium cucumbers, seeded
5 cups (1.25 litres) chicken stock
3 spring onions (scallions), roughly chopped
60 g (2 oz) butter
⅓ cup (1½ oz) flour
salt
freshly ground pepper
¼ cup (2 fl oz) cream
2 egg yolks
drop of green food colouring (optional)
thin cucumber slices for garnish

Cut cucumbers into 2.5 cm (1 in) pieces. Combine with the stock and spring onions in a large saucepan. Cover and simmer for 30 minutes or until the cucumber is soft. Push through a sieve and discard the skins.

Melt the butter in a large saucepan. Stir in the flour and cook for 1 minute. Remove the pan from heat and gradually add the cucumber stock. Stir continuously until the soup boils and thickens slightly. Season to taste with salt and a generous amount of pepper. Mix the cream and egg yolks together and stir through the soup. Add the green food colouring if desired.

Chill in the refrigerator until serving time. Arrange the cucumber slices on the soup and serve immediately.

PUMPKIN CHEESE SOUP (photograph on page 20)

Serves 6

One serve contains	
Carbohydrate	7 g
Calories	100
Kilojoules	420

500 g (1 lb) pumpkin, peeled and chopped
1 medium onion, finely chopped
2½ cups (20 fl oz) chicken stock
good pinch nutmeg
1 cup (4 oz) grated Cheddar cheese
salt
freshly ground black pepper
chopped parsley for garnish

Place the pumpkin, onion and stock in a large saucepan. Simmer gently until the pumpkin is cooked (about 20–30 minutes). Remove the pumpkin. Mash or purée then return to the liquid. Add the cheese and nutmeg; stir until the cheese has melted. Do not boil. Season with salt and pepper and serve garnished with chopped parsley and a little extra grated cheese if desired.

CHICKEN AND CORN CHOWDER

'Planned over' (planned to be left over) chicken is the base for this impressive meal in a soup.

Serves 6

One serve contains	
Carbohydrate	12 g
Calories	262
Kilojoules	1095

2 cups (16 fl oz) chicken stock
1 large or 2 medium potatoes, peeled and diced
1 medium carrot, diced
1 small onion, chopped
½ teaspoon salt
freshly ground black pepper
100 g (3½ oz) cooked chicken, diced
220 g (7 oz) creamed corn
spring onions (scallions) for garnish

Combine the stock, diced potato, carrot, onion, salt and pepper in a saucepan. Bring to the boil and simmer for 20 minutes.

Add the chicken and corn and cook for another 5 minutes. Pour into serving dishes and garnish with diagonally sliced spring onions.

POTAGE CRÈME DE CHAMPIGNONS

Serves 8

One serve contains	
Carbohydrate	11 g
Calories	240
Kilojoules	1005

500 g (1 lb) fresh mushrooms, trimmed and sliced
6 cups (1.5 litres) hot chicken stock
2 medium onions, chopped
90 g (3 oz) butter
½ cup (2 oz) flour
nutmeg
salt
freshly ground black pepper
1 cup (8 fl oz) cream
2 tablespoons lemon juice
chopped parsley for garnish

Reserve half a cup of mushrooms. Combine mushrooms, stock and onions in a large saucepan, simmer for 20 minutes. Purée in a blender or put through a sieve.

Melt the butter and stir in the flour. Remove from the heat and gradually add the mushroom stock, stirring constantly. Return to heat and stir until boiling. Season to taste with nutmeg, salt and pepper. Stir in the cream, lemon juice and reserved mushrooms (do not boil as the soup will curdle). Check seasoning and serve immediately garnished with parsley.

FIRST COURSES

As this is your guest's first impression of your menu, it is worthwhile taking a little trouble with this course. Remember a main course follows, so make the servings small and light. The first course should titillate the appetite, not satiate it.

Appetisers should have variety in flavour and texture. Serve both hot and cold food. Vary the shapes and sizes. Serve large and small morsels, chunks, triangles, balls, crescents and sticks. Most importantly, contrast their colours. If the food looks insipid, take extra time with garnishing to make it look 'appetising'.

Most of the recipes presented in this section can be prepared well before the party. Dips develop their best flavour if made ahead of time. Vary the size and shape of 'dippers', and for something different try shelled prawns, cheese cubes, pumpernickel or rye bread, chunks of fresh fruit and a large selection of vegetable sticks.

Dishes such as the Seafood Crepes, Bacon Stuffed Mushrooms and Prawn Toasts can all be refrigerated overnight and heated just before serving. Throughout the book there are recipes for more sustaining dishes that can also be served as first courses.

SEAFARERS' DIP

Left-overs make a delicious sandwich spread.

250 g (8 oz) ricotta cheese
170 g (5½ oz) canned salmon, drained
1 tablespoon chopped spring onions, (scallions)
1 teaspoon Worcestershire sauce
pinch cayenne pepper
pinch salt
extra chopped spring onions (scallions) for garnish

Total recipe contains	
Carbohydrate	6 g
Calories	594
Kilojoules	2490

Mix all of the ingredients together thoroughly and spoon into a small serving dish. Top with the extra spring onions (scallions) and serve surrounded with a variety of raw vegetable sticks (try celery, carrots, red or green peppers, cauliflowerettes, mushrooms and cucumber).

CORNY BACON DIP

2 slices lean bacon, trimmed and chopped
125 g (4 oz) canned creamed corn
250 g (8 oz) ricotta cheese, crumbled

Total recipe contains	
Carbohydrate	31 g
Calories	602
Kilojoules	2520

Sauté the chopped bacon in a small frying pan until crisp. Drain on absorbent paper. Combine the bacon (reserve 1 teaspoon for garnish), corn and ricotta cheese. Mix well.

Spoon the dip into a serving dish and top with the reserved bacon. Serve with vegetable sticks or crackers.

BATEAU BAY DIP

250 g (8 oz) creamed cottage cheese
¼ cup (2 oz) canned tuna, drained and flaked
¼ cup (2 oz) chopped asparagus spears
1 tablespoon chopped spring onions (scallions) or chives
dash Tabasco sauce
¼ teaspoon salt
freshly ground black pepper
pimento or parsley for garnish

Total recipe contains	
Carbohydrate	9 g
Calories	364
Kilojoules	1525

Combine all ingredients, mix well and chill. Garnish with pimento or parsley and serve with vegetable sticks or soya-flavoured rice crackers.

HERB STUFFED EGGS

Yields 12 appetisers

6 eggs, hard-boiled
1 tablespoon chopped chives
1 tablespoon chopped parsley
2 tablespoons sour cream
2 teaspoons lemon juice
¼ teaspoon curry powder
cayenne pepper to taste
salt
freshly ground black pepper
paprika and parsley for garnish

One serve contains	
Carbohydrate	neg.
Calories	42
Kilojoules	180

Peel eggs, cut in half lengthwise. Scoop out the yolks, mash, and mix with the remaining ingredients. Using 2 teaspoons, carefully spoon the mixture back into the hollow in the egg whites. Chill before serving sprinkled with paprika and garnished with parsley.

PRAWN TOASTS

Prawn Toasts can be prepared the day before and baked just before serving.

Makes 48

250 g (8 oz) raw prawn meat
2 slices bacon
¼ cup (1 oz) sliced water chestnuts
2½ tablespoons cornflour (cornstarch)
2 teaspoons dry sherry
2 eggs, lightly beaten
½ teaspoon salt
12 slices toast bread
flat-leafed parsley

One serve contains	
Carbohydrate	4 g
Calories	32
Kilojoules	135

Preheat the oven to 190°C (375°F/Gas 5). Chop prawn meat finely with a cleaver or heavy, sharp knife. Chop bacon and water chestnuts together as finely as possible. Combine prawns, bacon mixture, wine, eggs, cornflour and salt. Mix thoroughly to form a paste.

Cut crusts from bread, then cut each slice into quarters. With a knife or spatula, spread equal amounts of mixture on each piece of bread, mounding it slightly in the centre.

Arrange on oven trays and bake for 10 minutes. Serve hot or cold. Place a parsley leaf gently in the centre of each mound.

Courtesy of Bread Research Institute of Australia.

AVOCADO AND PRAWN COCKTAIL

Serves 6

One serve contains	
Carbohydrate	5 g
Calories	310
Kilojoules	1300

3 small ripe avocados, halved and stoned
250 g (8 oz) shelled, cooked prawns (shrimps)
⅓ cup (2½ fl oz) mayonnaise (see page 50)
2 cloves of garlic, crushed
juice of ½ lemon
coriander
nutmeg
salt
freshly ground black pepper
4 slices bacon, cooked until very crisp and crumbled

Scoop out the avocado flesh, leaving the skins intact. Set skins aside.

In a mixing bowl, mash the avocado flesh until smooth and creamy. Add the prawns, mayonnaise, garlic, lemon juice, coriander and nutmeg. Season to taste with salt and pepper. Mix gently until well combined.

Spoon the mixture back into the avocado shells. Sprinkle with crumbled bacon and serve immediately.

DIXON STREET CHICKEN WINGS

Yields 10 appetisers

One serve contains	
Carbohydrate	2 g
Calories	90
Kilojoules	380

10 chicken wings
2 tablespoons lemon juice
2 tablespoons soy sauce
2 tablespoons tomato sauce
1 teaspoon finely chopped green ginger
lemon slices and parsley for garnish

Place chicken wings in a glass or earthernware bowl. Combine remaining ingredients and pour over chicken. Cover, and marinate for at least 2 hours. Cook under a preheated griller (broiler) or barbecue for 15 minutes, turning and basting frequently. Remove to a serving platter and garnish with lemon slices and parsley.

CHICKEN LIVERS PROVENÇALE

Serves 6

One serve contains	
Carbohydrate	7 g
Calories	136
Kilojoules	570

2 slices bacon, trimmed and chopped
1 medium onion, chopped
1 clove garlic, crushed
250 g (8 oz) chicken livers, trimmed and coarsely chopped
125 g (4 oz) fresh mushrooms, quartered
500 g (1 lb) canned or fresh chopped tomatoes
bay leaf
½ teaspoon mixed herbs
salt
freshly ground black pepper
chopped parsley for garnish

Sauté the bacon, onion and garlic for about 5 minutes or until the onion is golden brown. Add the livers and fry a further 5 minutes or until browned on all sides. Add the mushrooms, cook for 1 minute. Stir in the tomatoes, bay leaf, herbs, salt and pepper. Cover, simmer gently for 20–25 minutes. Check seasoning.

Serve over brown rice in individual dishes. Garnish with parsley.

BACON STUFFED MUSHROOMS

Can be prepared before the day of your dinner party. To serve as a first course, use large open mushrooms and extend the cooking time for an extra 5–10 minutes or until just tender.

Yields about 30 appetisers

One appetiser contains	
Carbohydrate	1 g
Calories	30
Kilojoules	125

30 g (1 oz) butter
½ cup (1 oz) fresh breadcrumbs
310 g (10 oz) small fresh mushrooms
4 slices bacon, trimmed and chopped
1 medium onion, finely chopped
3 tablespoons chopped green pepper
½ teaspoon salt
freshly ground black pepper
125 g (4 oz) ricotta cheese
¼ cup (2 fl oz) hot water

Preheat the oven to 190°C (375°F/Gas 5). Melt the butter in a frying pan. Toss the breadcrumbs in the butter until lightly browned. Set aside.

Wipe over mushrooms. Remove and chop the stems. Sauté the chopped bacon, onion, green pepper, chopped mushroom stems, salt and pepper. Cook until just tender but not browned, about 15 minutes. Reduce the heat and stir in the ricotta cheese.

Put the mixture into the mushroom caps, making small mounds of stuffing. Lightly dip the tops of the stuffed mushrooms into the buttered breadcrumbs. Place the mushrooms, filling side up, in a baking dish. Cover and refrigerate until ready to use (they can be kept until next day if necessary).

Add the hot water to the baking dish and bake uncovered for 15–20 minutes. Serve garnished with sprigs of parsley.

CRAB QUICHES

Yields 15 crab quiches

One quiche contains	
Carbohydrate	10 g
Calories	206
Kilojoules	860

1 quantity wholemeal pastry (see page 114)
1 small onion, finely chopped
310 g (10 oz) crabmeat
3 eggs
1 egg yolk extra
1 cup (8 fl oz) milk
½ cup (4 fl oz) cream
cayenne pepper
salt
freshly ground pepper
1 cup (4 oz) grated Cheddar cheese
lemon slices and parsley sprigs for garnish

Preheat the oven to 190°C (375°F/Gas 5). Roll pastry out thinly, cut into rounds (use a fluted cutter if available), and press into shallow patty tins. Place onion and then the crabmeat evenly into each tartlet case.

Beat eggs, milk, cream, cayenne pepper, salt and pepper together. Pour over crabmeat, filling each case two-thirds full. Sprinkle with cheese and bake for 20 minutes or until the filling is set. Serve hot. Garnish serving platter with lemon and parsley.

ANTIPASTO (photograph opposite)

Translated literally from Italian, **antipasto** means 'before the meal'. It is an appetiser of spicy foods served as a first course at the table.

Serves 12

One serve contains	
Carbohydrate	10 g
Calories	292
Kilojoules	1220

470 g (15 oz) can artichoke hearts
250 g (8 oz) fresh button mushrooms
bottled Italian dressing
1 bunch radishes
crisp celery stalks
4 small tomatoes, sliced
2 small pickled beetroot, sliced
10 gherkins
6 hard-boiled eggs, halved
200 g (7 oz) black or green olives
125 g (4 oz) can pimentos, sliced
500 g (1 ib) cooked unshelled prawns
250 g (8 oz) Gruyèye cheese
250 g (8 oz) Gorgonzola cheese
Yoghurt Dressing for serving (see page 51)

Place drained artichoke hearts in a bowl, cover with Italian dressing and leave to marinate. Clean and trim mushrooms, place in another bowl and marinate in Italian dressing for 2 hours. Stir occasionally. Drain and chill. Wash and trim radishes; if desired cut into 'roses' and leave in iced water for 2 hours. Cut celery into 8 cm (3 in) lengths, make into curls if desired.

Arrange them and the other ingredients in an attractive pattern on a large serving platter. Serve with a bowl of Yoghurt Dressing and fresh crusty bread.

HAWAIIAN MEATBALLS

Yields 80 appetisers

One appetiser contains	
Carbohydrate	1 g
Calories	39
Kilojoules	165

750 g (1½ lb) lean minced beef
250 g (8 oz) lean minced pork
440 g (14 oz) can unsweetened pineapple, drained and crushed
2 sticks celery, finely chopped
2 medium carrots, finely grated
1 large onion, minced
3 teaspoons Worcestershire sauce
1 teaspoon salt
freshly ground black pepper
3 tablespoons oil

Preheat the oven to 180°C (350°F/Gas 4). Combine all the ingredients, except the oil in a mixing bowl. Mix well. Form mixture into small meatballs (keep your hands wet to prevent mixture sticking). Heat the oil in a frying pan, brown the meatballs on all sides.

Drain them and place on a baking tray. Bake for 15–20 minutes or until they are cooked. Serve the meatballs on toothpicks topped with a piece of pineapple, if desired.

Antipasto (page 36)

Carrot and Nut Collage Salad (page 44); Spinach Salad (page 47)

CAULIFLOWER BHAJI

Serves 4

One serve contains	
Carbohydrate	7 g
Calories	181
Kilojoules	760

500 g (1 lb) cauliflower
30 g (1 oz) butter
1 medium onion, chopped
2.5 cm (1 in) piece green ginger, finely chopped
1 teaspoon curry powder
½ teaspoon turmeric
1 teaspoon paprika
pinch chilli powder
1½ teaspoons salt
1 teaspoon garam masala

Break the cauliflower into sprigs, wash and drain thoroughly. Heat the butter in a large flameproof casserole. Sauté the onion and ginger until soft. Stir in the curry powder, turmeric, paprika and chilli powder. Add the cauliflower and cook, turning frequently for 5–10 minutes.

Add the salt, cover and simmer for about 20 minutes or until tender. Turn occasionally to give the cauliflower even colouring. Remove the lid and boil off most of the liquid. Sprinkle garam masala over cauliflower 5 minutes before end of cooking. Serve with steamed brown rice.

SALMON MOUSSE

Serves 8

One serve contains	
Carbohydrate	1 g
Calories	179
Kilojoules	750

2 teaspoons butter
1 small onion, chopped
440 g (14 oz) canned salmon
2 tablespoons lemon juice
1 tablespoon gelatine
¼ cup (2 fl oz) hot water
salt
dash Tabasco sauce
pinch nutmeg
¾ cup (6 fl oz) light sour cream, well chilled
¼ cup mayonnaise (see page 50)
1 egg white
Cucumber Mayonnaise for serving (see page 50)

Heat butter in a small frying pan; sauté the onion until soft. Remove the skin and bones from the salmon and place salmon with its liquid, onion and lemon juice in the bowl of a blender or processor; purée. Remove to a large bowl.

Dissolve the gelatine in hot water, cool and add to salmon with salt, Tabasco and nutmeg to taste. Whip sour cream until increased in volume, fold into salmon mixture with the mayonnaise. Beat egg white until stiff and fold into mixture with a metal spoon.

Pour into a lightly greased mould. Cover and refrigerate for several hours until set. Unmould on to a serving platter and garnish with salad vegetables. Serve with Cucumber Mayonnaise.

Note: 1 tablespoon Cucumber Mayonnaise adds 100 calories/420 kilojoules to a serve.

MUSHROOMS AND BACON IN BRANDY

One serve contains	
Carbohydrate	10 g
Calories	229
Kilojoules	960

Serves 4

3 slices lean bacon, roughly chopped
750 g (1½ lb) button mushrooms, trimmed and wiped
2 small tomatoes, peeled and chopped
freshly ground black pepper
2 tablespoons brandy
3 tablespoons cream
3 tablespoons grated Gruyère cheese
parsley sprigs for garnish

Preheat the oven to 180°C (350°F/Gas 4). Heat a large frying pan, fry the chopped bacon for 5 minutes and drain off excess fat. Add the mushrooms to the pan and cook, stirring frequently for 3–4 minutes or until the mushrooms are just tender, but still firm. Add the chopped tomato, pepper and brandy. Bring to the boil and simmer for 1 minute. Remove from the heat and stir in the cream.

Spoon the mixture into 4 ramekin dishes and sprinkle with grated cheese. Heat in the oven or under a griller (broiler) until the mushrooms are hot and the cheese has melted and is lightly browned. Garnish each with a parsley sprig and serve immediately.

ZUCCHINI MARINARA

Zucchini stuffed with prawns (shrimps) and tomatoes — a delectable start to any special meal.

One serve contains	
Carbohydrate	17 g
Calories	300
Kilojoules	1225

Serves 4

8 medium zucchini (courgettes) washed
salt
30 g (1 oz) butter
1 spring onion (scallion), chopped
1 clove garlic, crushed
3 large tomatoes, skinned and chopped
1 tablespoon Parmesan cheese
½ teaspoon chilli powder
salt
freshly ground black pepper
250 g (8 oz) fresh shelled prawns (shrimps), chopped if large
1 quantity Basic White Sauce (see page 51)
extra Parmesan cheese for topping
parsley for garnish

Preheat the oven to 200°C (425°F/Gas 7). Slice the zucchinis in half lengthwise. Carefully hollow out the flesh, leaving boat-shaped shells. Sprinkle salt into each shell and drain them on kitchen paper, hollow side down, for 20 minutes. Finely chop the scooped-out flesh. Heat the butter in a heavy-based frying pan. Sauté the spring onions and garlic until soft. Add the chopped zucchini flesh, tomatoes, Parmesan cheese, chilli, salt and pepper. Cook for 10 minutes or until it thickens. Add the prawns and reheat for 2 minutes.

Rinse and wipe zucchini halves with extra kitchen paper. Arrange skin-side down, in a well greased baking dish. Spoon a little of the tomato and prawn mixture into each shell. Spoon over the white sauce and sprinkle with extra Parmesan cheese.

Bake for 15–20 minutes or until it is piping hot and golden brown.

SEAFOOD CRÊPES

The perfect beginning for your dinner party — compliments will flow!

One serve contains	
Carbohydrate	26 g
Calories	499
Kilojoules	2090

Serves 6

Crêpes

1 cup (4 oz) sifted flour
pinch salt
3 eggs, lightly beaten
1½ cups (12 fl oz) milk
30 g (1 oz) butter, melted
clarified butter for cooking

Filling

45 g (1½ oz) butter
1 medium onion, finely chopped
125 g (4 oz) fresh mushrooms, sliced
¼ cup (1 oz) flour
250 g (8 oz) white fish fillets, poached and flaked
250 g (8 oz) peeled cooked prawns (shrimps), chopped
250 g (8 oz) scallops, poached in 1 cup (8 fl oz) milk and chopped
1 tablespoon dry sherry
pinch nutmeg
1 teaspoon salt
freshly ground pepper
1 cup (125 g) grated Cheddar cheese
lemon slices and parsley for garnish

Crêpes: Sift the flour and salt into a bowl, and make a well in the centre. Combine the remaining ingredients and gradually blend them into the flour, stirring continuously until smooth. To cook the crêpes, heat a little butter in frying pan (use only enough butter to cover the base, drain off excess). Pour in enough mixture to make a thin crêpe (about 2 tablespoons). Cook until the top appears bubbly, toss or turn with a slide. Cook for an extra minute. The side cooked first is served as the outer side. Stack crêpes and keep warm while making filling.

Filling: Poach the fish and scallops while making the crêpes. Melt the butter in a medium-sized saucepan. Sauté the onion and mushrooms until the onion is transparent. Stir in the flour, cook for 1 minute. Remove from the heat. Gradually blend in the milk from the scallops, stirring continuously. Return to the heat and stir until the sauce boils. Add more milk if the mixture is too thick. Simmer for a further 2 minutes. Add the flaked fish, prawns, scallops, sherry, nutmeg, salt and pepper.

To Assemble: Place 1–2 tablespoons filling on each crêpe. Roll up crêpes and place on a flat serving dish. Sprinkle with grated cheese. Place under a preheated griller or in the top half of the oven. Heat until cheese melts and crêpes are hot. Serve immediately garnished with lemon twists and sprigs of parsley. Accompany with a crisp side salad.

HAM AND CORN BLINTZES

Blintzes are related to crêpes; fillings used for crêpes can also be used for blintzes.

Serves 4

One serve contains	
Carbohydrate	25 g
Calories	494
Kilojoules	2070

Crêpes
1 cup (4 oz) wholemeal flour
2 eggs
1 cup (8 fl oz) water
½ teaspoon salt

Filling
2 cups (16 oz) cottage cheese
2 eggs
⅓ cup (2½ oz) corn kernels
¼ cup (2 oz) chopped ham
2 tablespoons Parmesan cheese
½ teaspoon salt
freshly ground pepper
60 g (2 oz) butter or margarine

Combine all ingredients for crêpes in a blender; blend until smooth. Set aside for 1 hour if possible.

To prepare the filling, blend the cottage cheese and eggs together. Stir in the corn, ham, cheese, salt and pepper.

Heat a lightly buttered crêpe pan (or a small frying pan) over medium heat. Pour about 3 tablespoons of the crêpe batter into pan. Quickly swirl pan to form a very thin crêpe to cover bottom of pan. When the underside has browned, turn crêpe out on to a cooling tray (cook one side only). Continue to cook the remaining batter.

Place about 2 tablespoons of the filling on centre of browned side. Fold sides in and roll up. Heat remaining butter in frying pan over medium low heat. Cook blintzes, seam side down, until golden brown. Serve immediately.

VEAL AND PORK TERRINE

Serves 12

One serve contains	
Carbohydrate	1 g
Calories	317
Kilojoules	1330

30 g (1 oz) butter
2 medium onions, chopped
1 clove garlic, crushed
1 kg (2 lb) pork and veal mince
3 eggs, lightly beaten
½ cup chopped parsley
2 teaspoons salt
sprig of fresh thyme, chopped
pinch ground cloves and nutmeg
freshly ground black pepper
¼ cup (2 fl oz) port
4 slices lean bacon
2 chicken breasts, flattened with a meat mallet
2 bay leaves

Preheat the oven to 180°C (350°F/Gas 4). Heat butter in a frying pan. Sauté the onions and garlic until soft.

In a large bowl combine the onions, mince, eggs, parsley, salt, thyme, cloves, nutmeg and a generous amount of pepper. Add the port and mix well. Place a layer of bacon in the base of an ovenproof dish, leaving enough to cover the top. Press half the meat mixture on to the bacon, cover with the thin chicken breasts and season with extra salt and pepper. Place remaining mince over the chicken and press down firmly. Cover with reserved bacon slices, top with bay leaves and cover with foil.

Put dish in a tray of water and bake for 1½ hours. Remove from water and place heavy weights on the top. Refrigerate for at least 8 hours before serving. Serve with Melba toast (thin pieces of bread, toasted) or fresh wholemeal bread and butter.

VEGETABLES, SALADS, SAUCES AND DRESSINGS

The ability to use basic ingredients to produce varied, interesting and nutritive menus is one of the marks of a successful cook. Vegetables are one of the best sources of vitamins and minerals and come in a large variety of flavours, colours and textures.

Select vegetables that are fresh and free from blemish. Most vegetables are at their best when eaten raw, but some must be cooked to be digested. Do not wash, soak or cut the vegetables until ready to cook. Place them in a minimum amount of boiling water and cook until just tender. Vegetables should not be cooked until their texture is mushy, as this impairs not only colour and flavour, but also most importantly the nutritive value. Formerly, it was common practice to add soda to the cooking liquid to intensify the colour of the vegetables. In fact, soda destroys ascorbic acid (Vitamin C) and renders the vegetables mushy. When boiling vegetables that grow underground such as potatoes, it is advisable to cover them. Leave above-ground vegetables uncovered.

In a country where vegetables are varied and plentiful don't be satisfied with just one type of salad greenery. Vary the lettuce — try cos or romaine, escarole, endive, mignonette or chicory. Grow your own watercress in the kitchen.

Wine, cider or herb-flavoured vinegars provide a subtle flavour to your salad dressings, or, if you prefer, lemon juice can be used in place of part or whole of the vinegar. Tarragon vinegar can be made by simply steeping the fresh or dried herb in the bottle of vinegar. Most salads improve if the dressings are added several hours before serving. Naturally, leafy greens such as lettuce, should be dressed at the last minute.

Despite the ever-increasing range of supermarket salad dressings, none can match the flavour of a fresh dressing specially made for the occasion. We have included Mayonnaise for the stalwarts yet for those with a sense of adventure, cottage cheese, yoghurt and sour cream can be the beginnings of great dressings. Yoghurt Dressing and Cottage Dressing have about one-third of the kilojoules of mayonnaise.

TOMATO AND GHERKIN SALAD

Serves 6

400 g (12½ oz) ricotta cheese, crumbled
2 medium tomatoes, chopped
2 gherkins, sliced
1 tablespoon chopped chives
1 stick celery, chopped
½ teaspoon salt
freshly ground black pepper
curly endive or lettuce leaves for serving

One serve contains	
Carbohydrate	4 g
Calories	87
Kilojoules	355

Lightly mix all ingredients together. Serve in a salad bowl lined with sprigs of endive or lettuce leaves.

EMERALD GREEN SALAD

Try serving this salad for lunch with Lebanese flat bread. This amount would make lunch for two.

Serves 4

One serve contains	
Carbohydrate	9 g
Calories	120
Kilojoules	500

1 tablespoon oil
125 g (4 oz) fresh mushrooms, sliced
¼ cup chopped fennel tops
1 cup (3½ oz) fresh green beans, cut into 2.5 cm (1 in) lengths
1 small onion, chopped
2 cloves garlic, crushed
¼ cup (1½ oz) chopped fennel bulb
1 small green pepper, roughly chopped
½ cup (1 oz) chopped celery
3 spring onions (scallions), chopped
¼ cup (1 oz) walnuts, halved
¼ cup (2 fl oz) bottled Italian dressing

Heat the oil in a heavy-based frying pan. Sauté the mushrooms, fennel tops, beans, onions and garlic until just tender. Allow to cool.

Add all remaining ingredients, mix well. Place in serving bowl, cover and refrigerate until serving time.

GREEK SALAD

Serves 8

One serve contains	
Carbohydrate	4 g
Calories	126
Kilojoules	525

1 lettuce, washed
4 tomatoes, cut into wedges
125 g (4 oz) feta cheese, cut into cubes
1 green pepper, sliced
chopped chives
10 black olives, pitted

Dressing

2 tablespoons lemon juice
2 tablespoons oil
1 clove garlic, crushed
pinch oregano
salt
freshly ground black pepper

Tear lettuce into bite-sized pieces. Combine with remaining ingredients in a large salad bowl. Toss with the dressing just before serving.

Dressing: Combine ingredients in a jar, shake well and pour over salad.

CARROT AND NUT COLLAGE SALAD

(photograph on page 38)

Serves 8

One serve contains	
Carbohydrate	16 g
Calories	106
Kilojoules	445

6 medium carrots, coarsely grated
½ cup (2 oz) raw peanuts or walnuts, roughly chopped
½ cup (1½ oz) bean sprouts
½ cup (3 oz) sultanas (seedless raisins)
3 tablespoons lemon juice

Combine all ingredients in a salad bowl, toss lightly to mix. If you are making this salad ahead of time, add the lemon juice just before serving.

MINTED POTATO SALAD

This salad is ideal for barbecues, picnics and buffets. The yoghurt and sour cream combination gives a sharp flavour with the consistency of mayonnaise but half the kilojoules.

Serves 8

One serve contains	
Carbohydrate	13 g
Calories	82
Kilojoules	345

6 medium potatoes
1 teaspoon salt
¼ cup bottled Italian dressing
3 tablespoons chopped chives
2 tablespoons chopped mint
freshly ground pepper
½ cup (4 fl oz) sour cream
⅓ cup (2½ fl oz) natural low fat yoghurt
sprigs of mint for garnish

Wash potatoes and cook slowly in gently boiling salted water until just tender. Cool. Peel and chop into 2 cm (¾ in) cubes. Sprinkle the potatoes with the Italian dressing to prevent discoloration.

Carefully mix in remaining ingredients. The best flavour can be achieved by adding the sour cream and yoghurt just before serving.

Garnish with sprigs of mint.

MARINATED ZUCCHINI SALAD

Serves 6

One serve contains	
Carbohydrate	4 g
Calories	18
Kilojoules	75

500 g (1 lb) fresh zucchinis (courgettes)
3 tablespoons finely chopped dill pickles
2 spring onions (scallions), chopped
2 tablespoons finely chopped red capsicum
1 tablespoon finely chopped parsley
½ cup (4 fl oz) bottled Italian dressing
salt
freshly ground black pepper
cos lettuce for serving

Wash and slice zucchinis into 1 cm (½ in) pieces. Cook in boiling salted water for 2–3 minutes (should be still quite crisp). Drain.

Remove to a bowl and add remaining ingredients except lettuce. Cover and marinate for several hours in the refrigerator. Serve in a salad bowl lined with cos lettuce leaves.

GREEN BEAN SALAD

Serves 6

One serve contains	
Carbohydrate	6 g
Calories	111
Kilojoules	465

2 tablespoons oil
500 g (1 lb) fresh green beans
¼ cup (2 fl oz) water
1 small onion, thinly sliced
1 clove garlic, crushed
½ cup (2 oz) grated Parmesan cheese
1 tablespoon chopped pimento or gherkin
1 tablespoon chopped parsley
bottled Italian dressing
few black olives and tomato wedges for garnish

Heat the oil in a large saucepan or frying pan with a lid. Sauté the beans for 5–10 minutes tossing to prevent them from burning. Add the water, cover and cook until tender but still crisp. Drain and cool quickly. Toss all ingredients together in a salad bowl. Chill until serving time.

Garnish with olives and tomato wedges.

PRAWN AND COLESLAW SALAD

Serves 4

One serve contains	
Carbohydrate	3 g
Calories	65
Kilojoules	270

90 g (3 oz) shelled cooked prawns (shrimps)
½ cup (1½ oz) shredded cabbage
1 medium carrot, grated
1 stick celery, diced
1 tablespoon Mayonnaise (see page 50)

Combine all ingredients in a salad bowl. Toss well and refrigerate until serving time.

FRUIT SLAW

Serves 6

One serve contains	
Carbohydrate	10 g
Calories	82
Kilojoules	345

2½ cups finely shredded cabbage
1 red apple, diced
1 small carrot, grated
3 tablespoons raisins
Thousand Island Dressing (see page 52)

Combine cabbage, apple, carrot and raisins in a salad bowl. Toss with dressing just before serving.

HAM AND MUSHROOM SALAD

Serves 8

One serve contains	
Carbohydrate	2 g
Calories	254
Kilojoules	1065

250 g (8 oz) lean ham, cut into strips
250 g (8 oz) fresh button mushrooms, sliced
250 g (8 oz) Emmenthal cheese, cut julienne style
Yoghurt Dressing (see page 51)

Combine ham, mushrooms and cheese in a large serving bowl. Pour over dressing, toss well and refrigerate until serving time.

BANANA AND YOGHURT RAITA

Banana and Yoghurt Raita is an Indian salad which is chilled and served as an accompaniment to curries.

Serves 6

One serve contains	
Carbohydrate	17 g
Calories	113
Kilojoules	475

2½ cups (20 fl oz) yoghurt
4 bananas, sliced
pinch chilli powder
1 tablespoon lemon juice
1 teaspoon garam masala
¼ teaspoon ground coriander
½ teaspoon salt
chopped fresh coriander for garnish

Mix the yoghurt until smooth. Add the remaining ingredients and pour into a serving dish. Cover and chill for 1 hour or until ready to serve.

Serve garnished with chopped coriander.

SPINACH SALAD (photograph on page 38)

Serves 6

½ bunch young spinach
2 oranges, segmented
75 g (2½ oz) button mushrooms, sliced
bottled Italian dressing
2 slices lean bacon, fried until crisp, then crumbled

One serve contains	
Carbohydrate	8 g
Calories	70
Kilojoules	295

Wash spinach, remove stems and tear into bite-sized pieces. Combine with the oranges and mushrooms in a salad bowl. Sprinkle with the dressing and chill. Top with crumbled bacon before serving.

AVOCADO AND MELON SALAD

This unusual salad is the perfect accompaniment to grilled lamb and beef, or it can be served as a first course. Chill the avocado and melon well before preparing the salad.

Serves 6 (or 4 as a first course)

2 medium avocados, halved and stoned
1 tablespoon lemon juice
½ medium honeydew melon, seeded

One serve contains	
Carbohydrate	8 g
Calories	181
Kilojoules	760

Dressing

3 tablespoons oil
3 tablespoons lemon juice
½ teaspoon salt
freshly ground black pepper
chopped fresh tarragon for garnish

With a small melon baller, scoop out the avocado flesh to within 3 mm (⅛ in) of the skin. Reserve the shells. Place the avocado balls in a bowl, sprinkle over the lemon juice. Set aside.

Scoop out the melon flesh in the same way and add to the avocado balls. Chill until nearly serving time. Pour over the dressing and gently toss the ingredients until well-coated.

Spoon the mixture into the avocado shells and sprinkle with the tarragon. Serve immediately.

Dressings: Combine all ingredients in a jar. Shake well just before using.

ANNA POTATOES

Serves 4

4 medium potatoes
45 g (1½ oz) butter
2 cloves garlic, crushed
1 teaspoon salt
freshly ground black pepper
½ cup (2 oz) grated cheese

One serve contains	
Carbohydrate	17 g
Calories	216
Kilojoules	905

Preheat the oven to 180°C (350°F/Gas 4). Peel and thinly slice the potatoes. Mix together the butter, garlic, salt and pepper. Place a layer of potatoes in the base of a small casserole dish. Dot with some of the butter mixture. Repeat the layers until completed, finishing with the grated cheese.

Cover and bake for 60–70 minutes or until the potatoes are tender. Remove the lid 20 minutes before the end of cooking to brown the top.

Serve straight from the casserole dish.

ROSEMARY POTATOES

Crushed rosemary leaves add a delicate pine flavour to the sautéed potatoes.

Serves 6

One serve contains	
Carbohydrate	17 g
Calories	107
Kilojoules	450

6 medium potatoes
1 teaspoon salt
30 g (1 oz) butter or margarine
2 cloves garlic, crushed
½ teaspoon dried or 1½ teaspoons fresh rosemary
freshly ground black pepper
chopped parsley for garnish

Par-boil potatoes in salted water; drain. Cut into 1 cm (½ in) slices.

Melt the butter in a large frying pan, sauté the garlic, rosemary and pepper. Add the potato slices and cook until golden brown on both sides. Present on a serving platter and sprinkle with parsley.

RATATOUILLE

A classic French vegetable casserole, Ratatouille (pronounced rah-tah-twee-y'h) is delightfully simple, yet delicious.

Serves 6

One serve contains	
Carbohydrate	7 g
Calories	94
Kilojoules	395

1 eggplant (aubergine)
salt
3 tablespoons oil
1 large onion, roughly chopped
2 cloves garlic, crushed
1 green pepper, cut into strips
4 medium zucchini (courgettes), cut into thick slices
3 tomatoes, peeled and roughly chopped
½ teaspoon oregano or mixed herbs
salt
freshly ground black pepper

Cut the eggplant into 1 cm (½ in) slices. Sprinkle with salt, leave for 30 minutes and pat dry with paper towels.

Heat the oil in a flameproof casserole. Sauté the onion and garlic until soft. Add the eggplant, green pepper and zucchinis and cook for a further 5–10 minutes. Stir in the tomatoes, herbs, salt and pepper. Cover and simmer gently for 25–30 minutes or cook in a moderate oven for 35–40 minutes. Be careful not to overcook as the vegetables will lose their shape and look unattractive.

Ratatouille may be served cold with crusty French bread as an hors-d'oeuvre or luncheon dish, or hot as an accompaniment to meat dishes.

TUSCONIAN SAUTÉ

Serves 4

One serve contains	
Carbohydrate	7 g
Calories	90
Kilojoules	375

2 tablespoons oil
125 g (4 oz) mushrooms, quartered
3–4 spring onions (scallions), chopped
2 zucchinis (courgettes), sliced
½ cup (4 fl oz) dry white wine
2 tomatoes, chopped
1 teaspoon salt
freshly ground black pepper

Heat the oil in a heavy based frying pan. Sauté the mushrooms, spring onions and zucchinis until tender. Be careful not to overcook as they will become mushy. Add the wine, allow to boil until the liquid evaporates. Stir in the chopped tomatoes, salt and pepper and cook a further 2 minutes.

Serve as an accompaniment to casseroles or grills.

CAULIFLOWER AND BACON BAKE

Serves 4

One serve contains	
Carbohydrate	14 g
Calories	249
Kilojoules	1040

1 small cauliflower
60 g (2 oz) bacon, trimmed and chopped
1 small onion, chopped
30 g (1 oz) butter or margarine
1½ tablespoons flour
1 cup (8 fl oz) milk
½ cup (2 oz) grated Cheddar cheese
salt
freshly ground white pepper
parsley for garnish

Preheat the oven to 180°C (350°F/Gas 4). Wash and trim the cauliflower. Break into small serving-sized pieces and steam over boiling salted water until almost tender. Remove to an ovenproof dish.

Sauté the bacon and onion until soft, about 5 minutes. Sprinkle over the cauliflower. Melt the butter in a medium saucepan. Stir in the flour and cook for 1 minute. Remove from heat and gradually add the milk, stirring continuously. Return to heat and stir until the sauce boils and thickens. Add half the grated cheese and season to taste with salt and pepper.

Pour over the cauliflower and sprinkle the remaining cheese over the top. Bake for 20 minutes or until golden brown. Garnish with parsley and serve immediately.

AUBERGINE PROVENÇALE

A vegetable accompaniment with a deliciots flavour. It will also serve as a hearty luncheon dish if served with brown rice and salad.

Serves 6

One serve contains	
Carbohydrate	10 g
Calories	182
Kilojoules	760

2 medium eggplants (aubergines)
2 tablespoons oil
1 medium onion, chopped
2 cloves garlic, crushed
125 g (4 oz) mushrooms, sliced
1 tablespoon tomato paste
500 g (1 lb) canned or fresh tomatoes, peeled and roughly chopped
½ cup (4 fl oz) dry white wine
½ teaspoon oregano
½ teaspoon basil
1 teaspoon salt
freshly ground black pepper
150 g (5 oz) mozzarella cheese, sliced

Preheat the oven to 180°C (350°F/Gas 4). Chop the eggplants into 2 cm (¾ in) pieces. Heat the oil in a large heavy-based saucepan. Cook the eggplants for 3–4 minutes. Remove to a greased casserole dish.

Sauté the onion, garlic and mushrooms until soft. Add the tomato paste, tomatoes, wine, oregano, basil, salt and pepper. Simmer for 10 minutes. Pour this tomato sauce over eggplants and top with cheese slices.

Bake for 30 minutes. Serve hot with grilled meat or fish.

MIDDLE-EASTERN TOMATOES

These stuffed tomatoes can be served as a first course, an accompaniment to grills or as a luncheon dish.

Serves 8

One serve contains	
Carbohydrate	24 g
Calories	332
Kilojoules	1390

8 firm tomatoes
salt
freshly ground black pepper
1 tablespoon oil
1 small onion, finely chopped
¼ cup (1 oz) pine nuts
¾ cup (4 oz) uncooked short grain rice
¾ cup (6 fl oz) hot water
3 tablespoons currants
1 tablespoon chopped mint
1 tablespoon chopped parsley
dry white wine or water

Preheat the oven to 180°C (350°F/Gas 4). Slice the tops from tomatoes and reserve them. Scoop out the tomato pulp keeping the shells intact. Place the tomato pulp, salt and pepper in a saucepan. Cook over a gentle heat until soft. Push through a sieve and set aside.

Heat the oil in a large saucepan. Sauté the onion until transparent. Add the pine nuts and cook a further 5 minutes. Stir in the rice, hot water, currants, mint and parsley. Bring to the boil, cover and simmer gently until all the liquid is absorbed (about 10 minutes). Season to taste with salt and pepper. Spoon the rice mixture into the tomato shells, leaving room for the rice to expand.

Replace tops and place tomatoes in a baking dish. Pour over the tomato purée with an equal quantity of white wine or water. Bake for 40–45 minutes. Serve hot or cold.

MAYONNAISE

To be sure of the success of this recipe, have the oil at room temperature adding it drop by drop to the egg mixture. Once the sauce begins to thicken, the rate may be increased. The quantity of oil used in mayonnaise makes it high in calories and kilojoules. An alternative for weight reducers would be Cottage Dressing.

Makes 1¼ cups

One tablespoon contains	
Carbohydrate	neg.
Calories	103
Kilojoules	430

2 egg yolks
½ teaspoon salt
freshly ground white pepper
½ teaspoon dry mustard
2 teaspoons lemon juice or white wine vinegar
1 cup (8 fl oz) oil

Place egg yolks in a mixing bowl, add salt, pepper, mustard and lemon juice. Whisk until smooth. Carefully add the oil, drop by drop, whisking continuously: the sauce will curdle if the oil is added too quickly. If this happens add a little extra vinegar and beat well.

As the mixture thickens, add the oil more quickly in a steady stream, whisking to prevent it from becoming too thick.

Use to combine ingredients in salads or serve with seafood.

Variations

Cucumber Mayonnaise: Add ¼ cup finely chopped cucumber and 1 teaspoon finely chopped fresh mint.

Mayonnaise With Fresh Herbs: Add 1–2 tablespoons chopped fresh herbs, such as chives, parsley, marjoram, thyme or basil.

BASIC WHITE SAUCE

The butter and flour combination (known as a 'roux') may be cooked and stored for future use. If the sauce becomes lumpy, stir briskly with a wire balloon whisk.

Yields 1 cup

Total recipe contains	
Carbohydrate	25 g
Calories	328
Kilojoules	1375

30 g (1 oz) butter
2 tablespoons flour
1 cup (8 fl oz) milk
(use half skim, half whole milk)
salt and pepper to taste

Melt the butter in a small saucepan over gentle heat. Stir in the flour and cook for 1–2 minutes. Remove from the heat and gradually add the milk. Return to the heat and stir until the sauce boils and thickens. Simmer for 1–2 minutes and season with the salt and pepper.

Variations

Cheese Sauce: Add ½ cup (2 oz) grated Cheddar cheese to the sauce. Stir until the cheese melts. (Carbohydrate 25 g; Calories 568).
Onion Sauce: Sauté 1 small chopped onion in the butter before adding the flour. (Carbohydrate 32 g; Calories 368).
Parsley Sauce: Add 2 tablespoons finely chopped parsley to the finished sauce. (Cabohydrate 25 g; Calories 328).

COTTAGE DRESSING

Use as a tangy low calorie substitute for mayonnaise.

Yields 2 cups

One tablespoon contains	
Carbohydrate	neg.
Calories	39
Kilojoules	160

1 cup (8 oz) cottage cheese
¾ cup (6 fl oz) sour cream
small clove garlic, crushed
2 teaspoons vinegar
½ teaspoon Worcestershire sauce
1 teaspoon dry mustard
½ teaspoon salt
¼ teaspoon pepper

Blend all of the ingredients together until smooth. Chill to develop the flavour before serving.

YOGHURT DRESSING

Yields 1½ cups

One tablespoon contains	
Carbohydrate	neg.
Calories	31
Kilojoules	130

½ cup (4 fl oz) natural yoghurt
⅓ cup (2½ fl oz) polyunsaturated oil
2 tablespoons white vinegar
⅓ cup snipped chives
2 tablespoons chopped parsley
1 clove garlic, crushed
½ teaspoon prepared mustard
few drops liquid artificial sweetener
1 teaspoon salt
freshly ground pepper

Combine all ingredients in a screw-top jar. Shake well and refrigerate until serving time. Shake before using.

BÉCHAMEL SAUCE

Yields 1¼ cups

Total recipe contains	
Carbohydrate	34 g
Calories	568
Kilojoules	2380

1¼ cups (10 fl oz) milk
(use half whole, half skim milk)
1 medium onion, quartered
1 carrot, sliced
1 stick celery, chopped
6 peppercorns
bay leaf
40 g (1⅓ oz) butter
2 tablespoons flour
salt

Combine milk, onion, carrot, celery, peppercorns, and bay leaf in a saucepan. Cover and heat gently for 30 minutes, then strain. Melt the butter in a saucepan, stir in flour with a wooden spoon. Cook for 1 minute.

Remove from heat, add all of the warm milk immediately, stirring constantly. Return pan to heat and stir until the sauce boils and thickens.

Variations

Mushroom Sauce: Add 125 g (4 oz) sautéed sliced mushrooms.
Caper Sauce: Add 2–3 tablespoons chopped capers to the finished sauce.

THOUSAND ISLAND DRESSING

Yields 1 cup

One teaspoon contains	
Carbohydrate	neg.
Calories	22
Kilojoules	90

½ cup (4 fl oz) polyunsaturated oil
2 tablespoons finely chopped onion
1 tablespoon chopped stuffed olives
1 tablespoon chopped parsley
1 tablespoon Worcestershire sauce
2 teaspoons lemon juice
1 tablespoon orange juice
½ teaspoon salt
pinch mustard
paprika

Combine all ingredients in a screw-top jar. Shake well before pouring over salads.

MAIN COURSES

Meat is one of the most popular protein foods. It is also one of the most expensive! As a result there is a swing towards alternatives such as fish, poultry and legumes which are all lower in fat and kilojoules, too.

Variety is the key to interesting family meals. Many of us fall into the rut of chops and three vegetables, so, next shopping day, discover some of the alternatives and incorporate them into your meal planning. Visit the fish markets, and as a starter try the Creole Fish and Potatoes or Sole en Papillote.

Vegetarian cookery does not necessarily mean bland, unappetising meals. The addition of herbs and spices turns even humble beans into interesting dishes. Those who are not vegetarians will also enjoy them.

Being lovers of garlic we always have a large supply with a garlic crusher nearby. After much use we have found an easy way to peel a clove of garlic (without getting garlicky fingers!) Place the clove concave-side down on a board. Now press down with your thumb on the centre of the clove. The skin should break away easily without the use of a knife. Onions are another all-time favourite. If they bring you to tears, store in the refrigerator to minimise the gases that are emitted during chopping. Alternatively, soak the peeled onions in cold water for 30 minutes before chopping. If your fingers do have the smell of garlic or onion, rub in salt and then wash in *cold* water.

LOBSTER CHÂTEAU

Serves 4

One serve contains	
Carbohydrate	2 g
Calories	240
Kilojoules	1005

2 x 1 kg (2 lb) cooked lobsters, shells split, claws cracked and grey sacs removed
60 g (2 oz) butter
1 teaspoon salt
freshly ground black pepper
¼ teaspoon cayenne pepper
½ cup (4 fl oz) brandy
3 teaspoons Beurre Manie (see page 67)

Remove the lobster meat from the shell; cut meat into cubes. Clean the shell halves and place in a heatproof dish and set aside. Melt the butter in a heavy frying-pan. When the foam subsides, add the lobster, salt, pepper and cayenne. Cook for 3–4 minutes or until lightly browned. Remove from heat.

Preheat the griller (broiler). Heat the brandy in a small saucepan, until hot but not boiling. Pour over the lobster meat and ignite with a match. Leave until the flames have died down. Remove the lobster meat from the pan and place in the reserved shells.

Return pan to heat and bring the liquid to the boil. Reduce the heat and gradually stir in the Beurre Manie, beating until the sauce thickens.

Pour the sauce over the lobster and place under griller for 5–10 minutes or until golden brown. Serve immediately with a tossed salad.

SWEET AND SOUR PRAWNS (photograph opposite)

Serves 4

One serve contains	
Carbohydrate	11 g
Calories	237
Kilojoules	990

315 g (10 oz) peeled fresh green prawns (shrimps)
1½ tablespoons flour
¼ cup (2 fl oz) polyunsaturated oil
1 medium onion, chopped
⅓ cup (1 oz) diced green pepper
1 tablespoon tomato purée
1 cup (8 fl oz) chicken stock
½ cup (4 fl oz) white vinegar
dash chilli sauce
1 teaspoon salt
2 teaspoons cornflour (cornstarch)
1 tablespoon pineapple juice (from pineapple pieces)
¼ cup (1½ oz) unsweetened pineapple pieces
2 medium tomatoes, cut into wedges
liquid artificial sweetener, if desired

Clean and de-vein prawns and coat with flour. Heat the oil, cook prawns (in two or three lots) until golden brown. Remove from pan and keep warm.

Drain off any excess oil. Sauté the onions until tender, then add the green pepper and cook 1 minute longer. Stir in the tomato purée, stock, vinegar, chilli sauce, and salt. Blend the cornflour with the pineapple juice and add to sauce. Stir until boiling, and leave to simmer for 2 minutes.

Add the tomatoes and pineapple pieces, re-heat and sweeten if necessary. Return prawns to pan, toss gently and serve immediately with steamed rice.

FISH BAKED WITH GINGER (photograph opposite)

Serves 4

One serve contains	
Carbohydrate	8 g
Calories	230
Kilojoules	965

4 whiting fillets
60 g (2 oz) butter or margarine
2 tablespoons soy sauce
1 tablespoon grated fresh green ginger
1 tablespoon lemon juice
salt
freshly ground pepper
2 large onions, thickly sliced
2 large tomatoes, sliced
lemon twists and parsley for garnish

Preheat the oven to 160°C (325°F/Gas 3). Place the fillets in a greased baking dish. Melt the butter, add the soy sauce, ginger, lemon juice, salt and pepper. Pour this sauce over the fish fillets. Top with alternate layers of sliced onion and tomato. Bake uncovered, for 20–25 minutes or until the fish is tender. Baste frequently during cooking.

Garnish with lemon twists and parsley and serve with steamed brown rice and tossed salad.

Fish Baked with Ginger (page 54); Sweet and Sour Prawns (page 54)

Crusty Roast Veal (page 84)

Mexican Steak (page 78); English Muffins (page 115)

Chump Chops with Chicken Livers (page 90)

SALMON QUICHE

Serves 6

One serve contains	
Carbohydrate	17 g
Calories	508
Kilojoules	2125

Pastry

½ cup (2 oz) sifted white flour
½ cup (2 oz) wholemeal flour
⅛ teaspoon salt
90 g (3 oz) butter or margarine
1 egg yolk
1 tablespoon lemon juice

Filling

4 slices bacon, trimmed and diced
250 g (8 oz) canned salmon
3 eggs
1½ cups (12 fl oz) cream
2 tablespoons chopped parsley
1 tablespoon grated Parmesan cheese
½ teaspoon paprika
1 teaspoon salt
freshly ground black pepper

Pastry: Preheat the oven to 190°C (375°F/Gas 5). Mix flours and salt together. Rub in the butter until the mixture resembles fine breadcrumbs. Add egg yolk and lemon juice and mix to a firm dough (if necessary, add a tablespoon of water). Press the pastry into a 25 cm (10 in) flan tin.

Filling: Gently fry bacon in a small frying pan. Drain on absorbent paper. Drain and flake salmon, reserve liquid. Arrange the salmon on the base of the pastry shell, sprinkle the bacon on top.

Beat together the reserved salmon liquid, eggs, cream, parsley, cheese, paprika, salt and pepper. Pour over the back of a spoon to cover the salmon and bacon.

Bake for 10 minutes in preheated oven then reduce heat to 160°C (325°F/Gas 3) and cook a further 30–35 minutes or until the filling has set.

FISH FILLETS WITH WINE AND MUSHROOM SAUCE

Serves 6

One serve contains	
Carbohydrate	16 g
Calories	303
Kilojoules	1270

1 kg (2 lb) fish fillets
¼ cup (1 oz) cornflour (cornstarch)
salt
freshly ground pepper
2 teaspoons curry powder
½ teaspoon garlic salt
250 g (8 oz) fresh mushrooms, sliced
½ cup (2½ oz) sultanas (seedless raisins)
½ cup (4 fl oz) dry white wine
2 tablespoons lemon juice
1 tablespoon Worcestershire sauce
few drops liquid artificial sweetener (optional)
30 g (1 oz) butter or margarine
lemon slices and parsley for garnish

Preheat the oven to 180°C (350°F/Gas 4). Cut fish fillets into serving-sized portions if large. Mix together the cornflour, salt, pepper, curry powder and garlic salt. Coat the fish fillets with this mixture. Place half the fish in a greased shallow ovenproof dish; add half the mushrooms and sultanas. Top with the remaining fish, mushrooms and sultanas.

Mix together the wine, lemon juice, Worcestershire sauce and sweetener, if desired. Pour over the fish. Dot with butter; cover with foil and bake for 50–60 minutes or until cooked (depending on the size of the fillets). Garnish with lemon slices and parsley and serve with brown rice.

SPANISH PAELLA

Paella (pronounced 'pay-ee-yah') is traditionally made from a combination of seafood, chicken, sausage, vegetables and rice. It varies from an inexpensive rice dish with a handful of prawns to an elaborate dish with lobsters and mussels. Our elaborate 'dinner party' version can be changed to your own taste. Prepare the ingredients before starting to cook.

Serves 8

One serve contains	
Carbohydrate	43 g
Calories	479
Kilojoules	2005

2 tablespoons oil
1 x 1 kg (2 lb) chicken, cut into small pieces
60 g (2 oz) Cabana sausage, sliced
1 medium onion, sliced
2 cloves garlic, crushed
3 tomatoes, peeled and chopped
1 red pepper, sliced
1 teaspoon salt
freshly ground black pepper
1 teaspoon paprika
2 cups (12 oz) long-grain rice, soaked in cold water for 30 minutes and drained
2½ cups (20 fl oz) chicken stock
¼ cup (2 fl oz) lemon juice
1 teaspoon saffron threads, soaked in 4 tablespoons hot water for 10 minutes to extract flavour and colour
90 g (3 oz) shelled peas
250 g (8 oz) king prawns (shrimps), shelled (reserve a few in shells for garnish)
1 x 750 g (1½ lb) lobster, shelled and cut into 2.5 cm (1 in) pieces
750 g (1½ lb) mussels, scrubbed, steamed then shelled (reserve a few in shells for garnish)

Heat the oil in a large flameproof casserole or paella pan. Add the chicken pieces and sausage, cook for 10–15 minutes or until the chicken is golden brown. Remove and set aside.

Add the onion and garlic to the pan, sauté until the onion is soft. Stir in the tomatoes, red pepper, salt, pepper and paprika. Cook until the mixture is thick.

Add the rice and, shaking the pan frequently, fry for 3 minutes or until the rice is transparent. Add the stock, lemon juice and saffron mixture. Bring to the boil, then reduce heat to low and stir in the peas. Return the chicken pieces and sausage slices to the pan, cook for 15 minutes, stirring occasionally.

Add the prawns, lobster and mussels and cook for a further 5 minutes or until the chicken is cooked and all the liquid has been absorbed. Serve immediately, garnished with the reserved prawns and mussels in their shells.

MUSSELS WITH RICE

Serves 6

One serve contains	
Carbohydrate	33 g
Calories	258
Kilojoules	1080

3 tablespoons oil
2 medium onions, chopped
2 cups (16 oz) mussels, cleaned and shelled
4 cups (1¼ lb) cooked brown rice
1 cup (8 fl oz) beef stock
¼ cup (1½ oz) raisins
1 tablespoon grated fresh green ginger
½ teaspoon salt
freshly ground black pepper
parsley sprigs for garnish

Heat the oil in a large frying pan with a lid. Sauté the onions until transparent. Add the mussels and cook a further 2 minutes. Mix in the rice, stock, raisins, ginger, salt and pepper.

Cover and simmer for 15 minutes. check seasoning and serve immediately garnished with parsley.

TROUT AMANDINE

Serves 4

One serve contains	
Carbohydrate	8 g
Calories	398
Kilojoules	1665

4 medium-sized trout
3 tablespoons flour
1 teaspoon salt
freshly ground black pepper
60 g (2 oz) butter
60 g (2 oz) flaked almonds
¼ cup (2 fl oz) lemon juice
1 tablespoon chopped parsley

Wash and scale trout, pat dry with kitchen paper. Open the fish out as flat as possible (skin side up). Run a bottle or rolling pin firmly down the backbone before boning the fish. Turn fish over and using a sharp knife gently lever out the backbone. Remove any other bones that may remain. Press the fish back into shape. Coat with the seasoned flour.

Heat half the butter in a large frying pan. Cook the trout until golden brown on both sides, about 8–10 minutes. Remove to serving platter and keep warm while making the sauce.

Heat remaining butter until frothy. Add the almonds, and sauté gently until lightly browned.

Add the lemon juice, stirring to lift any sediment in the pan. Simmer until nearly all the lemon juice has evaporated. Stir in the parsley and pour over the trout. Serve immediately.

CHINATOWN FILLETS

Serves 4

One serve contains	
Carbohydrate	2 g
Calories	309
Kilojoules	1295

4 (about 1 kg) gemfish fillets (or use any firm-fleshed white fish)
juice and rind of 2 lemons
2 tablespoons soy sauce
2 tablespoons oil
2 cloves garlic, crushed
2.5 cm (1 in) piece green ginger, finely chopped
lemon twists and chopped parsley for garnish

Marinate the fish fillets for at least 1 hour in the lemon juice, rind and soy sauce. Heat the oil in a heavy-based frying pan. Sauté the garlic and ginger for 1 minute.

Add the fish fillets and cook gently for 6–8 minutes turning only once or twice. The fish should flake easily (do not overcook as the fish will toughen and dry out). Garnish with lemon twists and chopped parsley and serve with salad.

PARCELLED POISSONS

The fish fillets are baked in foil to trap the flavours of the tomato, onion and green pepper.

Serves 4

One serve contains	
Carbohydrate	7 g
Calories	226
Kilojoules	945

2 medium tomatoes, skinned and sliced
salt
freshly ground pepper
4 fish fillets
lemon juice
2 teaspoons Worcestershire sauce
2 medium onions, thinly sliced
1 green pepper, sliced into rings
chopped parsley
20 g (⅔ oz) butter or margarine

Preheat the oven to 200°C (400°F/Gas 6). Place the sliced tomatoes on four squares of heavy aluminium foil (shiny side in). Lightly sprinkle with salt and pepper. Place a fillet of fish on each square and squeeze over lemon juice. Sprinkle with Worcestershire sauce and extra salt and pepper. Top with onion and green pepper rings. Sprinkle with parsley. Dot with butter and seal packages well.

Bake for 20 minutes. Serve with rice or potatoes and salad.

BAKED SNAPPER

Serves 4

One serve contains	
Carbohydrate	12 g
Calories	388
Kilojoules	1625

1 x 1.5 kg (3 lb) whole snapper
1 onion, finely chopped
½ green pepper, chopped
1½ cups (7 oz) cooked rice (approx. ½ cup raw)
1 stick celery, finely chopped
salt
freshly ground black pepper
60 g (2 oz) butter
¼ cup (2 fl oz) lemon juice
½ cup spring onions (scallions), chopped
1 tablespoon grated green ginger
1 teaspoon soy sauce
1 lemon, thinly sliced
chopped parsley for garnish

Preheat the oven to 160°C (325°F/Gas 3). Wash and scale fish. Mix together onion, green pepper, rice, celery, salt and pepper. Pack stuffing firmly into the fish. Place fish in a well-greased baking dish.

Melt the butter in a saucepan. Remove from heat and add the lemon juice, spring onions, ginger and soy sauce. Season with extra salt and pepper. Pour sauce over the fish and bake for 40–50 minutes or until cooked. Baste with the sauce frequently during cooking.

Remove fish to a serving platter, pour pan juices over them. Place lemon slices down the centre of the fish and sprinkle with chopped parsley.

CREOLE FISH AND POTATOES

An economical family dish.

Serves 4

One serve contains	
Carbohydrate	22 g
Calories	289
Kilojoules	1210

2 tablespoons oil
1 medium onion, sliced
3 medium potatoes, sliced thinly
1 tablespoon flour
500 g (1 lb) canned or fresh tomatoes, roughly chopped
1½ teaspoons salt
freshly ground black pepper
500 g (1 lb) fish fillets
chopped parsley for garnish

Heat the oil in a large heavy frying pan with a lid. Add the onion and potatoes and cook gently for 10 minutes. Turn occasionally during cooking. Stir in the flour, then add the tomatoes, salt and pepper. Cover and cook until the potatoes are almost tender, about 20 minutes.

Place the fish on top of the potatoes, cover and cook further 15–20 minutes or until the fish is cooked. Garnish with chopped parsley and serve with green vegetables.

SOLE EN PAPILLOTE

Fillets of sole parcelled with mushrooms and prawns.

Serves 4

One serve contains	
Carbohydrate	2 g
Calories	221
Kilojoules	925

1 large or 2 small whole sole, cleaned and scaled
20 g (⅔ oz) butter
30 g (1 oz) mushrooms, sliced
½ small onion, finely chopped
¼ cup (2 fl oz) dry sherry
2 teaspoons cornflour (cornstarch)
2 tablespoons cold water
1 tablespoon lemon juice
180 g (6 oz) shelled cooked school prawns (shrimps)
1 tablespoon chopped parsley for garnish

Preheat oven to 180°C (350°F/Gas 4). Fillet the fish, carefully removing all the bones. Cut into 4 pieces.

Melt the butter in a saucepan or frying pan. Sauté the mushrooms until soft. Add the onion and sherry, and cook for 1 minute longer. Blend the cornflour with the cold water and stir into the mushrooms. Bring to the boil and simmer for 1 minute. Add the lemon juice.

Place each fillet of fish on individual greased squares of foil (double foil for added strength). Top with the prawns. Turn the sides of the foil up around the fish and carefully pour in the mushroom sauce. Wrap the fish parcels securely.

Bake for 30 minutes or cook over a barbecue for 20 minutes or until tender. Serve the fish in the foil. Open each parcel and sprinkle with the chopped parsley. Serve with a selection of salads.

SMOKED FISH WITH PASTA

Serves 4

One serve contains	
Carbohydrate	34 g
Calories	343
Kilojoules	1435

300 g (9½ oz) smoked cod or haddock
1 tablespoon vinegar
180 g (6 oz) wholemeal spaghetti
30 g (1 oz) butter
1 tablespoon grated Parmesan cheese
2 tablespoons chopped parsley
salt
freshly ground black pepper
2 eggs, beaten

Place smoked fish in a frying pan, cover with hot water and the vinegar. Poach for 15 minutes or until the fish flakes easily.

Meanwhile cook the spaghetti until tender. Drain, then add the flaked fish, butter, cheese, parsley, salt and pepper. Stir gently until hot. Add the beaten eggs, cook for another minute, then serve immediately with a tossed salad.

SMOKED FISH SOUFFLÉ

So light and elegant to serve at your next formal dinner party.

Serves 4

One serve contains	
Carbohydrate	9 g
Calories	353
Kilojoules	1480

250 g (8 oz) smoked cod or haddock fillets
1 cup (8 fl oz) milk
½ teaspoon salt
freshly ground black pepper
½ teaspoon paprika
pinch nutmeg
45 g (1½ oz) butter
3 tablespoons flour
¾ cup (3 oz) grated matured Cheddar cheese
1 tablespoon lemon juice
4 egg yolks
5 egg whites

Preheat the oven to 180°C (350°F/Gas 4). Place the fish in a frying pan with a lid. Pour over the milk, salt, pepper, paprika and nutmeg. Cover, simmer gently until the fish is cooked (about 10 minutes). Flake, retain liquid. Melt the butter in a saucepan. Stir in the flour and cook for 2 minutes.

Remove from heat and gradually add the fish liquor, stirring continuously. Stir in the grated cheese and lemon juice. Cook over a low heat until the cheese melts and the sauce is smooth and thick. Beat in the egg yolks one at a time, beating well after each addition. Carefully mix in the flaked fish.

Whisk the egg whites until stiff peaks form. Lightly fold into the fish mixture, being careful not to overmix. Pour into an ungreased soufflé dish and bake for 40–45 minutes. Serve immediately with a tossed salad.

POULTRY

SAUTÉED CHICKEN WITH BRANDY SAUCE

Serves 4

One serve contains	
Carbohydrate	1 g
Calories	341
Kilojoules	1425

4 chicken fillets
1 teaspoon salt
1 teaspoon freshly ground black pepper
60 g (2 oz) butter or margarine
3 spring onions (scallions), chopped
2 cloves garlic, crushed
¼ cup (2 fl oz) brandy
½ cup (4 fl oz) dry white wine
chopped spring onions (scallions) for garnish

Slice the chicken fillets into half horizontally to make 8 thin pieces. Rub all over with the salt and pepper. Set aside.

Melt the butter in a flameproof casserole. Sauté the spring onions and garlic for 1–2 minutes. Add the chicken fillets and brown on both sides. Pour over the brandy and wine, bring to the boil, stirring occasionally. Cover and simmer for 5–10 minutes or until tender. Transfer the chicken pieces to a warm serving dish. Keep warm while you finish sauce.

Boil the sauce for 3–5 minutes or until reduced by half. Pour sauce over the chicken and serve immediately garnished with chopped spring onions. Serve with Rosemary Potatoes (see page 48) and steamed vegetables.

CHICKEN SUPRÊME IN MUSTARD SAUCE

Serves 6

One serve contains	
Carbohydrate	11 g
Calories	237
Kilojoules	990

Chicken

30 g (1 oz) butter or margarine
4 spring onions (scallions), chopped
2 tablespoons chopped parsley
6 chicken breasts, skinned and boned
1 teaspoon salt
freshly ground white pepper

Sauce

45 g (1½ oz) butter or margarine
5 spring onions (scallions), chopped
¼ cup (1 oz) wholemeal flour
¾ cup (6 fl oz) evaporated skim milk
¾ cup (6 fl oz) dry white wine
1 tablespoon French mustard
1 teaspoon salt
freshly ground white pepper
extra parsley for garnish

Chicken: Heat the butter in a flameproof casserole. Sauté the spring onions and parsley for 1 minute. Add the chicken breasts and cook until golden brown on both sides. Season with salt and pepper. Reduce heat, cover and cook for 5 minutes or until tender.

Sauce: Heat the butter in a saucepan and sauté the spring onions for 1–2 minutes. Stir in the flour and cook 2 minutes longer. Remove from the heat. Gradually add the milk then the remaining ingredients. Return to heat and cook a few minutes longer until it has thickened.

To serve, place the chicken suprêmes in a shallow serving dish and pour the sauce over. Garnish with parsley, and accompany with new potatoes and steamed green vegetables.

GOLDEN DRUMSTICKS (photograph on page 2)

4 small servings

4 chicken drumsticks
50 g (1½ oz) potato crisps
30 g (1 oz) tasty Cheddar cheese, finely grated
½ teaspoon paprika

One serve contains	
Carbohydrate	6 g
Calories	205
Kilojoules	860

Preheat the oven to 180°C (350°F/Gas 4). Remove the skin from the chicken drumsticks. Crush the potato crisps and mix with the grated cheese and paprika. Press on to the chicken pieces. Place the drumsticks on a greased baking tray (sprinkle with any extra cheese mixture). Bake uncovered for 40–50 minutes.

Decorate with cutlet frills and serve hot or cold with salad. This dish is ideal for picnics.

BAKED SPICY CHICKEN

The yoghurt lends an unusual twist to the baked chicken pieces — a tasty alternative to rich cream.

Serves 4

4 large chicken pieces
1 cup (8 oz) natural low fat yoghurt
1 tablespoon chopped parsley
1 clove garlic, crushed
½ teaspoon chilli powder
½ teaspoon ground cardamon
¼ teaspoon cinnamon
¼ teaspoon ginger
1¼ teaspoons salt

One serve contains	
Carbohydrate	3 g
Calories	249
Kilojoules	1040

Place the chicken, skin side up, in an attractive baking dish. Combine the yoghurt, parsley, garlic, spices and salt. Pour over the chicken, cover and marinate for several hours, preferably overnight.

Preheat the oven to 180°C (350°F/Gas 4). Bake chicken for 1½ hours or until tender. Baste occasionally. Serve with pumpkin and green vegetables.

DEVILLED CHICKEN

The chicken pieces may also be cooked under a hot griller or wrapped in foil and cooked slowly on a barbecue.

Serves 4

4 chicken pieces
1¼ cups (10 fl oz) fresh orange juice
1 tablespoon grated orange rind
½ teaspoon dry mustard
½ teaspoon nutmeg
1 teaspoon curry powder
1 chicken stock cube, crumbled
salt
freshly ground pepper

One serve contains	
Carbohydrate	6 g
Calories	244
Kilojoules	1020

Place the chicken in a baking pan. Combine the remaining ingredients and pour over the chicken pieces. Marinate for 4–5 hours.

Preheat the oven to 180°C (350°F/Gas 4). Bake the chicken pieces for 1 hour or until they are tender. Baste frequently during cooking. Serve with saffron rice and a selection of salads.

GINGERED CHICKEN

Serves 4

One serve contains	
Carbohydrate	13 g
Calories	372
Kilojoules	1560

1 x 1.5 kg (3 lb) chicken
2 tablespoons soy sauce
1 teaspoon salt
2.5 cm (1 in) cube root ginger, chopped
2 tablespoons dry sherry
2 tablespoons oil
2 cloves garlic, crushed
¾ cup (6 fl oz) water
440 g (14 oz) unsweetened pineapple pieces with juice
1 tablespoon cornflour (cornstarch)
parsley for garnish

Mix the soy sauce, salt, ginger and sherry together. Pour over the chicken and allow to stand for at least 30 minutes. Turn occasionally.

Heat the oil in a large frying pan. Add garlic and brown the chicken on all sides. Add the marinade, water and juice from pineapple. Cover and simmer for 60 minutes or until the chicken is tender.

Cut the chicken into serving pieces and arrange on a serving platter. Cover and keep warm.

Add the pineapple pieces to the sauce. Thicken with the cornflour blended with a little water. Bring to the boil and spoon over the chicken pieces. Garnish with parsley. Serve with rice and a tossed salad.

COQ AU VIN

Serves 4

One serve contains	
Carbohydrate	10 g
Calories	609
Kilojoules	2550

1.5 kg (3 lb) chicken pieces
15 g (½ oz) butter
1 tablespoon oil
4 slices bacon, trimmed and chopped
6 small whole onions
2 cloves garlic, crushed
125 g (4 oz) fresh button mushrooms, trimmed
2 tablespoons brandy
1½ cups (12 fl oz) red wine
bouquet garni
1 teaspoon salt
freshly ground black pepper
Beurre Manie (see below)
parsley for garnish

Preheat the oven to 180°C (350°F/Gas 4). Dry the chicken pieces with paper towels. Heat the butter and oil in a heavy-based frying pan. Brown the chicken on both sides and remove to a casserole dish. Sauté the bacon, onion and garlic until the onion is transparent. Add the mushrooms and cook for 5 minutes longer. Pour over brandy and ignite, flame for about 1 minute then extinguish with wine. Add the bouquet garni, salt and pepper and pour the sauce over the chicken pieces.

Cover and bake for 1 hour or until the chicken is tender. Remove the bouquet garni and thicken the casserole with a little Beurre Manie. Garnish with parsley and serve with vegetables.

Beurre Manie

30 g (1 oz) butter
3 tablespoons (1 oz) flour

Beat butter and flour together. Add gradually to cooked casseroles, stirring until thickened as desired. Store leftovers in the refrigerator until required.

CHICKEN AND LEEK CASSEROLE

Serves 4

One serve contains	
Carbohydrate	10 g
Calories	502
Kilojoules	2100

1.5 kg (3 lb) chicken pieces
2 tablespoons flour
60 g (2 oz) butter
1 clove garlic, crushed
2 medium onions, chopped
2 carrots, sliced
2 sticks celery, chopped
½ cup (4 fl oz) dry white wine
2 cups (16 fl oz) chicken stock
1 teaspoon salt
freshly ground black pepper
125 g (4 oz) mushrooms, sliced
2 leeks, sliced

Coat the chicken pieces with flour. Heat the butter in a large flameproof casserole or saucepan. Sauté the garlic lightly then add the chicken pieces. Fry until golden brown. Remove from the pan.

Add the onions, carrots and celery to the pan, sauté until the onion is soft. Pour in the wine, then stock, salt and pepper. Return the chicken to the pan, cover and simmer for 40 minutes. Add the sliced mushrooms and leeks and cook for a further 30 minutes or until the chicken is tender. Serve with vegetables.

CHICKEN AND WALNUT BROCHETTES

Marinated skewered chicken served with the yoghurt marinade as a tangy sauce.

Serves 4

One serve contains	
Carbohydrate	9 g
Calories	304
Kilojoules	1275

4 chicken fillets
1 cup (5 oz) ground or finely chopped walnuts
½ cup (4 fl oz) lemon juice
4 spring onions (scallions), chopped
¼ cup (2 fl oz) chicken stock
2 cloves garlic, crushed
salt
freshly ground pepper
200 g (6½ oz) carton low-fat natural yoghurt, at room temperature
lemon and parsley for garnish

Remove skin from chicken and cut flesh into cubes. Place in a glass bowl.

Mix together walnuts, lemon juice, spring onions, stock, garlic, salt and pepper. Pour over chicken, mix well and leave to marinate for 3–4 hours. Stir occasionally.

Thread the chicken cubes on to skewers. Cook under a preheated griller (broiler) for 8–10 minutes or until cooked but not dry. Mix the marinade and yoghurt together and serve as an accompanying sauce. Garnish with lemon wedges and parsley sprigs and serve immediately.

VEGETARIAN

VEGETARIAN LASAGNE

Serves 6

One serve contains	
Carbohydrate	50 g
Calories	490
Kilojoules	2050

250 g (8 oz) wholemeal lasagne noodles
1 tablespoon oil
2 medium onions, chopped
4 cloves garlic, crushed
2 cups (14 oz) canned tomatoes, chopped
2 teaspoons oregano
1 teaspoon basil
3 tablespoons chopped parsley
salt
freshly ground black pepper
250 g (8 oz) mushrooms, sliced and lightly sautéed in butter
1 cup (6 oz) cooked red kidney beans (use canned or cooked dried beans)
2 cups (16 oz) cottage cheese
½ cup (2½ oz) grated Parmesan cheese
250 g (8 oz) mozzarella cheese, thinly sliced

Cook the lasagne noodles in a large saucepan of boiling salted water until just tender, about 10–15 minutes. Cover with cold water to prevent further cooking. Set aside.

Heat the oil in a large saucepan. Sauté the onion and garlic until soft. Add the tomatoes, oregano, basil, parsley, salt and pepper. Cook for 25–30 minutes until the mixture has thickened. Stir in the sautéed mushrooms and the red beans.

To assemble: Preheat oven to 190°C (375°F/Gas 5). Place a layer of the lasagne noodles in a baking dish. Cover with a third of the tomato sauce, cottage and Parmesan cheese and mozzarella slices. Repeat layers until all the ingredients are used, finishing with mozzarella slices. Bake for 30 minutes. Remove from oven 5 minutes before serving. Serve with a tossed salad.

SPINACH WITH MACARONI

Serves 4

One serve contains	
Carbohydrate	41 g
Calories	403
Kilojoules	1690

1 cup (5 oz) wholemeal macaroni
1 bunch spinach
4 tablespoons rolled oats
1 cup (250 ml) tomato juice
1 tablespoon soy sauce
1½ cups (6 oz) grated Cheddar cheese
salt
freshly ground black pepper

Preheat the oven to 190°C (375°F/Gas 5). Cook the macaroni in boiling salted water until tender. Drain. Meanwhile wash and chop the spinach; cook in 1 cup boiling water. Using a slotted spoon, remove spinach to a casserole dish and reserve liquid. Add the oats and tomato juice to the spinach liquid. Simmer for 10 minutes. Remove from heat and add the soy sauce, 1 cup of the cheese and salt and pepper.

To assemble, place the macaroni on top of the spinach. Pour over the sauce and sprinkle with remaining ½ cup cheese. Place in top half of the oven for 20 minutes or until heated through.

CANNELONI STUFFED WITH SPINACH

Serves 6

One serve contains	
Carbohydrate	29 g
Calories	422
Kilojoules	1765

1 tablespoon oil
1 medium onion, chopped
6 large ripe tomatoes, chopped
½ cup (4 fl oz) dry white wine
½ cup (4 fl oz) chicken stock
2 teaspoons mixed herbs
salt
freshly ground black pepper
½ bunch spinach
500 g (16 oz) ricotta cheese
2 eggs
½ cup (2 oz) Parmesan cheese
nutmeg
salt and pepper
12 canneloni tubes
250 g (8 oz) mozzarella cheese, thinly sliced

Preheat the oven to 190°C (375°F/Gas 5). Heat the oil in a saucepan. Sauté the onion until soft. Add the tomatoes, wine, stock, herbs, salt and pepper. Simmer for 20 minutes or until quite thick. Purée if desired.

Meanwhile, wash the spinach and remove the stalks. Cook in a little salted water until just tender. Drain and chop. Add the ricotta cheese, eggs, Parmesan cheese, nutmeg, salt and pepper.

Cook the canneloni tubes according to directions on the packet. Drain and rinse in cold water to stop sticking. Fill the canneloni tubes with the spinach mixture. Place side by side in a single layer in a greased shallow dish. Pour over tomato sauce and top with the cheese slices. Bake for 20 minutes or until hot. Serve with a side salad.

SPINACH LASAGNE

A delightful alternative to a meat-based lasagne.

Serves 6

One slice contains	
Carbohydrate	70 g
Calories	560
Kilojoules	2345

½ x 350 g (11 oz) packet green lasagne noodles
1 bunch spinach
pinch nutmeg
90 g (3 oz) butter
½ cup (2 oz) flour
3 cups (24 fl oz) milk
½ cup (2 oz) grated cheese
salt
freshly ground pepper
125 g (4 oz) mozzarella cheese, sliced

Cook lasagne noodles according to directions on the packet. Place in cold water and set aside. Meanwhile, wash the spinach. Discard stalks and roughly chop leaves.

Place in saucepan with nutmeg and just enough water to cover bottom of pan. Cover and boil for 5 minutes. Remove from heat, drain off water. Place in a blender or processor, blend until smooth.

Melt the butter in a saucepan, stir in the flour and cook for 1 minute. Remove from heat, gradually add the milk, stirring constantly. Return pan to heat and stir until the sauce boils and thickens. Add the cheese, salt and pepper, stir until the cheese has melted. Remove from heat.

To assemble: Place a layer of noodles in a shallow ovenproof dish. Spread with half the spinach purée, then cover with one-third of the cheese sauce. Top with second layer of noodles, then spinach, another third of the cheese sauce, remaining noodles and finish with cheese sauce.

Arrange mozzarella cheese slices over the top and bake in a moderate 180°C (350°F/Gas 4) oven for 25–30 minutes or until golden brown. Serve with tossed salad and garlic bread.

SPINACH AND RICOTTA PIE

The unusual combination of rolled oats and cheese in the base highlights the creamy spinach filling.

Serves 6 (or 8 as a first course)

One serve contains	
Carbohydrate	14 g
Calories	311
Kilojoules	1300

Base

1 cup (3 oz) rolled oats
1 cup (4 oz) grated Cheddar cheese
¼ teaspoon paprika

Filling

2 eggs
2 cups chopped cooked spinach
250 g (8 oz) ricotta cheese, crumbled
½ cup (2 oz) grated Cheddar cheese
¼ teaspoon nutmeg
½ teaspoon salt
freshly ground black pepper
extra ½ cup (2 oz) grated Cheddar cheese

Base: Preheat the oven to 180°C (350°F/Gas 4). Mix the oats, cheese and paprika together, press into a well-greased 20 cm (8 in) pie dish.

Filling: Lightly beat the eggs. Mix in the spinach, ricotta, grated cheese, nutmeg, salt and pepper. Spoon the mixture into the pie crust and sprinkle with the extra grated cheese. Bake for 30–35 minutes.

PLEASURE PIE

Serves 6

One serve contains	
Carbohydrate	30 g
Calories	384
Kilojoules	1605

1½ tablespoons wheatgerm
1 tablespoon butter
3 medium onions, quartered
1 cup (8 fl oz) skim milk
1 cup (5 oz) cooked brown rice
2 eggs, beaten
300 g (9½ oz) canned mixed beans, drained
2 teaspoons mixed herbs
1 tablespoon Worcestershire sauce
salt
freshly ground pepper
1 cup (4 oz) grated Cheddar cheese

Preheat the oven to 190°C (375°F/Gas 5). Lightly grease a round casserole dish; sprinkle with wheatgerm. Heat the butter in a frying pan and sauté the onions until golden brown. Mix them together with the milk, rice, beaten eggs, beans, herbs, sauce, salt, pepper, and half of the cheese.

Turn the mixture into the prepared casserole and sprinkle with the remaining cheese. Bake for 30 minutes or until the custard is set and the top has browned. Allow to stand for 10 minutes before serving. Cut into wedges and serve hot or cold with salad.

GARDEN VEGETABLE PIE

Use 'planned-over' vegetables from the night before for this pie. Try a mixture of cooked pumpkin, onion, potato, celery, cauliflower, peas or any of your choice.

Serves 4

One serve contains	
Carbohydrate	51 g
Calories	462
Kilojoules	1935

Base
2 cups (10 oz) cooked brown rice
¼ cup (1 oz) Parmesan cheese
¼ cup (1½ oz) ground sesame seeds
1 egg, lightly beaten
1 teaspoon mixed herbs

Filling
4 cups (1¼ lb) cooked vegetables, chopped
1 tablespoon oil
250 g (8 oz) fresh mushrooms, quartered
1 clove garlic, crushed
3 tablespoons wholemeal flour
1 cup (8 fl oz) milk
1 tablespoon chopped parsley
⅛ teaspoon oregano
¼ teaspoon marjoram
1 teaspoon salt
freshly ground black pepper
½ cup (2 oz) grated Cheddar cheese

Preheat the oven to 180°C (350°F/Gas 4).

Base: Mix together rice, cheese, sesame seeds, egg and herbs. Press into a 20 cm (8 in) pie dish.

Filling: Place cooked vegetables in pie crust. Heat the oil in a large saucepan. Sauté the mushrooms and garlic until tender but not soft. Stir in the flour and cook for 2 minutes longer. Remove from heat and gradually add the milk. Return to heat and stir until the sauce thickens. Add the herbs, salt and pepper.

Pour the mushroom sauce over the vegetables and sprinkle with grated cheese. Bake for 30 minutes or until hot and bubbly. Serve with a side salad.

CRUSTY CORN SOUFFLÉ

Serves 4

One serve contains	
Carbohydrate	27 g
Calories	300
Kilojoules	1255

60 g (2 oz) butter
¼ cup (1 oz) flour
440 g (14 oz) canned creamed corn
4 eggs, separated
1 tablespoon grated Parmesan cheese
1 tablespoon chopped parsley
1 teaspoon salt
freshly ground black pepper
parsley for garnish

Preheat the oven to 180°C (350°F/Gas 4). Melt the butter in a medium-sized saucepan. Stir in the flour and cook for 1 minute. Remove from heat and add the creamed corn. Add the egg yolks, one at a time, beating well after each addition.

Mix in the cheese, parsley, salt and pepper. Beat the egg whites until stiff peaks form, fold lightly into the mixture until just combined. Pour into an ungreased soufflé dish and bake for 45–50 minutes. Garnish with parsley and serve immediately.

ONION CHEESE SOUFFLÉ

Serves 4

One serve contains	
Carbohydrate	12 g
Calories	356
Kilojoules	1490

½ cup (2 oz) finely grated Parmesan cheese
2 medium onions
1 tablespoon butter
3 tablespoons flour, sifted
½ teaspoon dry mustard
½ teaspoon salt
freshly ground black pepper
1 cup (8 fl oz) skim milk
1 cup (4 oz) grated tasty cheese
4 eggs, separated
paprika

Preheat the oven to 200°C (400°F/Gas 6). Lightly grease a soufflé dish and dust the base and sides evenly with the Parmesan cheese. If not using the cheese, leave the soufflé dish ungreased. Finely slice the onions, separate into rings and reserve about ½ cup.

Sauté remaining onion in the butter until lightly browned. Sprinkle in the flour, mustard, salt and pepper, cook for 1 minute. Remove from heat and gradually add the milk, stirring constantly. Return to heat, add the cheese and continue stirring until the cheese melts.

Add the egg yolks one at a time, beating well after each addition. Beat the egg whites until stiff peaks form. Lightly fold the cheese mixture into the whites until just combined. Be careful not to overmix, as this will cause a heavy soufflé. Pour into the prepared soufflé dish. Arrange the reserved onion rings over the top and sprinkle with paprika. Bake for 40–45 minutes. Serve immediately with a crisp side salad.

MUSHROOM AND LENTIL PIE

Even without the pastry, the pie filling is delicious for an easily prepared meal to serve four.

Serves 6

One serve contains	
Carbohydrate	52 g
Calories	337
Kilojoules	1410

180 g (6 oz) red lentils
3 cups (24 fl oz) beef stock
1 bay leaf
¾ teaspoon salt
1 tablespoon oil
2 medium onions, chopped
2 cloves garlic, crushed
250 g (8 oz) fresh mushrooms, chopped
1 quantity Potato Pastry (see page 114)

Pie: Preheat the oven to 180°C (350°F/Gas 4). Combine the lentils, stock, bay leaf and salt in a saucepan. Cover and simmer for 20 minutes or until the water is absorbed and the lentils are soft. Remove bay leaf.

Meanwhile, heat the oil in a frying pan. Sauté the onion, garlic and mushrooms until just tender. Mix the lentils and mushroom mixture together. Set aside.

Pastry: Reserve one-third of the pastry for the top. Line a 23 cm (9 in) pie dish with the remaining pastry. Fill the pie with the mushroom filling. Roll out the reserved pastry, place on top of the pie and press edges to seal. Cut a small hole in the centre to allow steam to escape while cooking. Brush the top with a little milk. Bake for 30–40 minutes or until crisp and golden brown.

Variation

Mushroom and lentil casserole: Omit pastry. Pour filling into a casserole and sprinkle with ¼ cup (½ oz) wholemeal breadcrumbs and ¼ cup (1 oz) grated Cheddar cheese. Serves 4. (Carbohydrate 63 g; Calories 285.)

CABBAGE AND NUT LOAF

Serves 6

One serve contains	
Carbohydrate	21 g
Calories	396
Kilojoules	1660

2 tablespoons oil
2 large onions, chopped
2 cloves garlic, crushed
4 cups (12 oz) shredded cabbage
2 cups (8 oz) chopped walnuts
1 cup (2 oz) fresh wholemeal breadcrumbs
1 tablespoon soy sauce
1 teaspoon nutmeg
4 eggs, lightly beaten
½ cup (4 fl oz) milk
salt
freshly ground pepper
extra ½ cup (1 oz) fresh breadcrumbs
1 teaspoon mixed herbs
1 tablespoon Parmesan cheese

Preheat oven to 180°C (350°F/Gas 4). Heat the oil in a large saucepan and sauté the onion and garlic until soft. Add the cabbage and cook for a further 5 minutes. Mix in walnuts, breadcrumbs, soy sauce, nutmeg, beaten eggs and milk. Season to taste with salt and pepper. Press into a greased loaf tin.

Mix together extra breadcrumbs, herbs and cheese, sprinkle over loaf. Bake for 25–30 minutes or until piping hot and golden brown.

CABBAGE STRUDEL (photograph opposite)

Sautéed cabbage and bacon rolled in crisp golden pastry.

Serves 4

One serve contains	
Carbohydrate	21 g
Calories	508
Kilojoules	2125

60 g (2 oz) butter or margarine
2 medium onions, finely chopped
4 slices bacon, trimmed and chopped
¼ fresh cabbage, finely shredded (optional)
1 teaspoon caraway seeds
salt
freshly ground black pepper
2 hard-boiled eggs, chopped
3 tablespoons cottage cheese
½ packet filo pastry
oil for pastry

Preheat the oven to 180°C (350°F/Gas 4). Melt the butter in a heavy-based frying pan. Sauté the onions and bacon (if using) until soft. Add the cabbage and cook for 3 minutes longer. Mix in caraway seeds and season to taste with salt and pepper. Remove mixture to a bowl and fold in chopped eggs and cottage cheese.

Brush oil between pastry sheets and place in a stack. Top with cabbage mixture and roll up. Seal the edges, place on a greased oven tray and bake for 30 minutes. Serve with a tossed salad.

Cabbage Strudel (page 74)

Tournedos Chasseur (page 78)

TOMATO AND EGGPLANT CASSEROLE

Serves 6

One serve contains	
Carbohydrate	32 g
Calories	438
Kilojoules	1835

2 x 470 g (15 oz) cans tomatoes
½ teaspoon basil
¼ teaspoon oregano
1 teaspoon salt
freshly ground black pepper
125 g (4 oz) ribbon noodles
30 g (1 oz) butter
2 tablespoons oil
2 large onions, chopped
1 large eggplant, cut into 2.5 cm (1 in) cubes
2 cloves garlic, crushed
1 red pepper, sliced
1 green pepper, sliced
3 sticks celery, chopped
250 g (8 oz) fresh mushrooms, sliced
2 cups (8 oz) grated mozzarella cheese
1 cup (4 oz) grated Cheddar cheese
½ cup (2 oz) fresh breadcrumbs
chopped parsley for garnish

Preheat the oven to 180°C (350°F/Gas 4). Combine undrained tomatoes, basil, oregano, salt and pepper in a saucepan. Roughly mash the tomatoes and simmer uncovered for 30 minutes or until it becomes a thick sauce. Meanwhile, cook noodles in boiling salted water until just tender. Drain, then place in cold water to prevent noodles sticking.

Heat butter and oil in a large frying pan. Add the onions, eggplant, garlic, peppers, celery and mushrooms, sauté until the onions are tender.

Mix together the sautéed vegetables, tomatoes, noodles and mozzarella cheese. Season to taste. Pour into a large greased casserole dish and sprinkle with the Cheddar cheese and breadcrumbs. Cover and bake for 40 minutes; increase the oven temperature to 200°C (400°F) and bake uncovered, for 10 minutes longer. Garnish with chopped parsley and serve with a tossed salad.

SOUFFLÉ TOMATO BAKE

A cheese and rice soufflé with a baked tomato base.

Serves 4

One serve contains	
Carbohydrate	12 g
Calories	371
Kilojoules	1555

3 medium tomatoes, peeled and thickly sliced
30 g (1 oz) butter
⅓ cup (1½ oz) flour
1 cup (8 fl oz) milk
180 g (6 oz) grated Cheddar cheese
½ cup (2½ oz) cooked brown rice
3 eggs, separated
½ teaspoon salt
freshly ground white pepper
mustard
tomato wedges and parsley for garnish

Preheat the oven to 200°C (400°F/Gas 6). Place the tomato slices into a round casserole dish.

Melt the butter in a saucepan. Stir in the flour and cook for 1 minute. Remove from the heat and gradually add the milk. Return to the heat and stir until the sauce boils and thickens. Remove the pan from heat once again and stir in the cheese, rice, egg yolks, salt, pepper and mustard. Beat the egg whites until stiff, lightly fold into mixture until only just combined (be careful not to overmix as the soufflé will be heavy).

Pour mixture over tomatoes and bake for 35 minutes. Serve immediately garnished with the tomato wedges and parsley, and accompanied by a side salad.

BEEF

MEXICAN STEAK (photograph on page 57)

Serves 4

One serve contains	
Carbohydrate	17 g
Calories	309
Kilojoules	1295

1 tablespoon oil
1 medium onion, chopped
1 large clove garlic, crushed
500 g (1 lb) round steak, cubed
1 red or green pepper, chopped
1 stick celery, sliced
½ teaspoon chilli powder
1 tablespoon flour
½ cup (4 fl oz) red wine
2 medium tomatoes, peeled and chopped
1 bay leaf
½ teaspoon salt
freshly ground black pepper
150 g (5 oz) canned red kidney beans, drained
3 tablespoons tomato paste
parsley for garnish

Heat the oil in a large saucepan. Sauté the onion, garlic and steak. Add the red pepper and celery and cook for 2 minutes longer. Mix in the chilli powder and flour, then add the wine, tomatoes, bay leaf and salt. Cover and simmer gently for 30–40 minutes or until the meat is tender.

Stir in the kidney beans and tomato paste, then re-heat. Remove the bay leaf. Serve on a bed of rice garnished with parsley.

TOURNEDOS CHASSEUR (photograph on page 76)

Serves 4

One serve contains	
Carbohydrate	1 g
Calories	261
Kilojoules	1095

2 teaspoons oil
60 g (2 oz) fresh mushrooms, sliced
2 spring onions (scallions), chopped
1 teaspoon cornflour (cornstarch)
½ cup (4 fl oz) beef stock
1 teaspoon tomato paste
½–1 teaspoon salt
freshly ground black pepper

Tournedos

4 x 2.5 cm (1 in) thick tournedos (buy 500 g (1 lb) beef fillet)
½ cup (4 fl oz) dry white wine

Heat the oil in a heavy-based saucepan. Sauté the mushrooms and spring onions. Stir in the cornflour, cook over a low heat for 1 minute. Add the remaining ingredients and simmer for 10–15 minutes.

Tournedos: Meanwhile, heat a lightly greased frypan. Cook the tournedos over a high heat for 2–3 minutes on each side. Remove to a warm serving dish. Drain off excess fat.

Add the wine to the pan, stirring to loosen the brown sediment on the bottom of the pan. Reduce the liquid by half and add the chasseur sauce. Bring to the boil and pour over the tournedos. Garnish with extra sautéed sliced mushrooms. Serve with jacket potatoes and a tossed endive salad.

STEAK DIANE

Serves 4

One serve contains	
Carbohydrate	1 g
Calories	217
Kilojoules	910

1 tablespoon butter
2 cloves garlic, crushed
500 g (1 lb) fillet steak, cut thinly and flattened with a meat mallet
salt
freshly ground black pepper
¼ cup (2 fl oz) water
1 tablespoon tomato sauce
1 teaspoon Worcestershire sauce
1 teaspoon cornflour (cornstarch)
1 tablespoon finely chopped parsley

Heat the butter in a large frying pan. When beginning to froth add the garlic and steaks. Cook steaks for 1 minute or more on each side (depending on how well done you require them). Remove steaks from pan, season with salt and pepper and keep warm while making sauce.

Add the water and sauces to the pan; stir to lift the sediment. Thicken with the cornflour blended with a little water. Bring to the boil then add the chopped parsley. Pour the sauce over the steaks and serve immediately with new boiled potatoes and a choice of other vegetables.

GOURMET MEATBALLS

Serves 6

One serve contains	
Carbohydrate	17 g
Calories	477
Kilojoules	1995

750 g (1½ lb) lean minced beef
1½ cups (3 oz) fresh breadcrumbs
1 small onion, chopped
1 egg
½ teaspoon dry mustard
2 tablespoons chopped parsley
1 tablespoon Worcestershire sauce
¼ cup (2 fl oz) milk
½ teaspoon salt
freshly ground black pepper
30 g (1 oz) butter or margarine
1 medium onion, chopped
2 tablespoons flour
2 cups (16 fl oz) beef stock
⅓ cup (2½ fl oz) red wine
220 g (7 oz) canned sliced mushrooms

Preheat the oven to 190°C (375°F/Gas 5). Mix together the minced beef, breadcrumbs, onion, egg, mustard, parsley, sauce, milk, salt and pepper. Form the mixture into 2.5 cm (1 in) balls and place in a lightly greased casserole. Bake for 35–40 minutes or until cooked.

Meanwhile, prepare the sauce. Melt the butter in a heavy-based saucepan. Sauté the onion until transparent. Stir in the flour and cook for 1 minute. Remove from the heat and blend in the stock and wine. Return to the heat and stir until boiling. Add the mushrooms and pour over the meatballs. Bake for 5 minutes longer and serve.

STIR-FRIED BEEF

Serves 4

One serve contains	
Carbohydrate	8 g
Calories	325
Kilojoules	1360

500 g (1 lb) rump or fillet steak
½ bunch spring onions (scallions)
1 tablespoon oil
1 clove garlic, crushed
½ teaspoon salt
1 tablespoon dry sherry
2 teaspoons soy sauce
2 tablespoons oyster sauce
½ cup (4 fl oz) beef stock
5–6 drops liquid artificial sweetener (optional)
1 tablespoon cornflour (cornstarch)
¼ cup (2 fl oz) water

Trim fat from the steak; slice across the grain into thin strips. Cut the spring onions diagonally into 2 cm (¾ in) lengths.

Heat the oil in a wok or frypan. Add spring onions, garlic and salt. Stir fry steak for 2–3 minutes; cooking small amounts at a time. Return to wok, add the sherry and soy sauce, and cook for 1 minute.

Stir in the oyster sauce, beef stock, sweetener if desired, and the cornflour blended with the water. Bring to the boil and serve immediately, garnished with spring onion flowers. Serve with steamed rice.

ORIENTAL BEEF

The steak is easily cut into fine strips if partially frozen.

Serves 4

One serve contains	
Carbohydrate	7 g
Calories	328
Kilojoules	1375

1 tablespoon oil
500 g (1 lb) round steak, cut into fine strips
1 cup (250 ml) water
250 g (8 oz) fresh green beans, sliced
1 medium carrot, cut into thin strips
2 sticks celery, chopped
1 large onion, chopped
cornflour (cornstarch)
soy sauce

Heat the oil in a large frying pan with a lid. Brown the meat on all sides. Add the water, cover tightly and steam for 5 minutes. Stir in the carrots and beans, steam for another 5 minutes. Thicken with a little cornflour blended with water. Add soy sauce to taste. Serve with brown rice.

FOIL-WRAPPED STEAK

Serves 6

One serve contains	
Carbohydrate	23 g
Calories	391
Kilojoules	1635

750 g (1½ lb) piece of rump steak, cut 3 cm (1¼ in) thick
1 packet dried oxtail (or beef) soup
1 teaspoon mustard
2 teaspoons mixed herbs
freshly ground black pepper
2 medium onions, sliced
2 medium carrots, sliced
2 tablespoons Worcestershire sauce
12 pitted prunes
30 g (1 oz) butter or margarine
2 tablespoons chopped parsley

Preheat the oven to 200°C (400°F/Gas 6). Place the steak on a large square of greased aluminium foil, with the shiny (reflecting) side next to the meat. Sprinkle the meat with the soup, mustard, herbs and peppers. Top with the onion and carrot slices and sprinkle with Worcestershire sauce. Arrange the prunes around the sides of the meat. Dot with butter and seal firmly to prevent the juices escaping (wrap twice if necessary).

Place on a baking tray and bake for 1½–2 hours or until the steak is tender. Open the foil for serving and sprinkle with the chopped parsley. Serve surrounded with vegetables.

POT-AU-FEU

A casserole of beef, mushrooms and celery with a crisp, golden topping of sliced potatoes.

Serves 4

One serve contains	
Carbohydrate	31 g
Calories	443
Kilojoules	1855

500 g (1 lb) blade or round steak, trimmed
2 tablespoons flour
1½ teaspoons salt
freshly ground black pepper
500 g (1 lb) potatoes
125 g (4 oz) mushrooms, trimmed and quartered
2 sticks celery, sliced
1 large onion, sliced
1 cup (8 fl oz) beef stock
30 g (1 oz) butter, melted

Preheat the oven to 180°C (350°F/Gas 4). Cut the steak into 2.5 cm (1 in) cubes and coat with flour seasoned with salt and pepper. Slice enough of the potatoes to cover the top of the casserole dish to be used. Cut the remainder into cubes. Mix together the cubed potatoes, mushrooms and celery. Place a layer of the sliced onion in the base of the casserole dish, cover with a layer of meat then mixed vegetables. Repeat layers and sprinkle over any remaining flour. Finish with the layer of overlapping sliced potatoes. Pour over the beef stock and brush the top with the melted butter.

Cover and cook for 1½ hours. Remove the lid and cook for a further 30 minutes to allow the top to crisp. Serve with a tossed salad or green vegetables.

SPAGHETTI BOLOGNAISE

Serves 4

One serve contains	
Carbohydrate	68 g
Calories	640
Kilojoules	1925

500 g (1 lb) lean minced (ground) beef
2 slices bacon, trimmed and chopped
1 medium onion, chopped
1 clove garlic, crushed
¾ cup (6 fl oz) dry red or white wine
4 fresh or 1½ cups canned tomatoes, chopped
4 tablespoons tomato paste
½ teaspoon oregano
½ teaspoon mixed herbs (or 1 tablespoon fresh)
1 teaspoon salt
freshly ground black pepper
250 g (8 oz) wholemeal spaghetti
Parmesan cheese for serving

Combine beef, bacon, onion and garlic in a large saucepan. Cook, stirring continuously until the meat is brown. Add the wine, tomatoes, tomato paste, oregano, herbs, salt and pepper. Mix well. Cover and simmer gently for 1 hour or until the meat is tender. Check seasoning.

Meanwhile, cook the spaghetti in boiling salted water until just tender (al dente). Serve bolognaise sauce on the spaghetti. Sprinkle with Parmesan cheese and serve with a tossed salad.

PORCUPINE MEATBALLS

When cooked, the expanded rice gives the meatballs a porcupine appearance. Perfect for buffets.

Serves 4

One serve contains	
Carbohydrate	36 g
Calories	517
Kilojoules	2165

½ cup (3 oz) uncooked rice
500 g (1 lb) minced (ground) beef
1 small onion, minced
2 tablespoons finely chopped green pepper
1 clove garlic, crushed
1 teaspoon salt
2 cups (16 fl oz) condensed tomato soup
1 tablespoon Worcestershire sauce
4 whole cloves
½ teaspoon cinnamon
¼ teaspoon liquid artificial sweetener

Combine the rice, minced beef, onion, green pepper, garlic and salt in a large bowl. Mix well and form into 3 cm (1¼ in) diameter balls.

Heat the soup, Worcestershire sauce, cloves, cinnamon and sweetener in a large saucepan. Drop in meatballs, cover tightly and simmer for 30 minutes or until the rice is cooked. Serve them with the sauce poured over.

PINWHEEL MEAT LOAF

Serves 8

One serve contains	
Carbohydrate	13 g
Calories	450
Kilojoules	1885

1 kg (2 lb) lean minced beef
1 egg, lightly beaten
3 tablespoons tomato sauce
1½ teaspoons salt
½ teaspoon freshly ground black pepper
1½ cups (3 oz) fresh breadcrumbs
1 small onion, finely chopped
1 teaspoon mixed herbs
salt and pepper
1 medium tomato, cut into thin wedges
3 slices lean bacon, cut in halves crosswise
2 tablespoons tomato sauce for topping
parsley for garnish

Preheat the oven to 190°C (375°F/Gas 5). Mix together the minced beef, egg, tomato sauce, salt and pepper. Turn out onto a large piece of foil and press into a 30 x 23 cm (12 x 9 in) rectangle.

Combine the breadcrumbs, onion, herbs, salt and pepper. Mix well and moisten with a little water. Spread over the meat.

Arrange the tomato wedges down one of the longer sides. Roll as for Swiss roll, peeling off the foil. Place seam-side down on a greased baking dish. Arrange the bacon rashers on top and bake for 1 hour. In the last 15 minutes of cooking, brush with the extra tomato sauce. Remove to a serving dish and garnish with parsley. Serve with steamed vegetables and mashed potatoes.

BOBOTIE

A traditional South African dish increasing in popularity throughout the world.

Serves 6

One serve contains	
Carbohydrate	21 g
Calories	631
Kilojoules	2640

1 tablespoon oil
2 medium onions, chopped
1 kg (2 lb) lean minced beef
1 slice brown bread
½ cup (4 fl oz) milk
1 tablespoon curry powder
1 teaspoon salt
freshly ground black pepper
2 teaspoons turmeric
½ cup (3 oz) chopped raisins
rind and juice of 1 lemon
2 tablespoons chopped almonds
2 tablespoons chutney
2 eggs
4 bay leaves
extra ½ cup (4 fl oz) milk

Preheat the oven to 180°C (350°F/Gas 4). Heat the oil in a large frying pan. Sauté the onions until they are golden brown. Add the meat and cook until browned. Soak the bread in the milk, then squeeze out. Add the minced beef, milk, curry powder, salt, pepper, turmeric, raisins, lemon, almonds, chutney and 1 egg.

Place the mixture in a buttered oven-proof dish. Push the narrow end of the bay leaves into the mixture so that they stand upright. Bake for 1 hour. Beat the extra egg and milk together; pour over the meat and bake for a further 30 minutes. Serve with boiled rice.

STEAK IN PEPPERS

Peppers stuffed with a succulent mixture of beef, bacon, mushrooms, onion and garlic.

Serves 4

One serve contains	
Carbohydrate	7 g
Calories	380
Kilojoules	1590

4 large green peppers
1 tablespoon oil
6 slices lean bacon, chopped
1 medium onion, chopped
125 g (4 oz) mushrooms, sliced
1 clove garlic, crushed
375 g (12 oz) lean minced beef
1 bay leaf
½ cup (4 fl oz) beef stock
dash Worcestershire sauce
salt
freshly ground black pepper

Blanch the peppers in rapidly boiling water for 2–3 minutes. Remove from the water, cut the tops off the peppers and remove the seeds.

Heat the oil in a flameproof casserole. Sauté the bacon, onion, mushrooms and garlic until the onion is soft. Remove and set aside. Add the minced beef to the casserole and brown well. Return mushroom mixture to the casserole. Add the bay leaf, stock, Worcestershire sauce, salt and pepper. Cover and simmer for 20 minutes or until the meat is tender. Remove the bay leaf and skim off any excess fat.

Preheat the oven to 180°C (350°F/Gas 4). Stuff the peppers with the cooked filling. Replace the tops and place in a baking dish. Pour ½ cup water into dish and bake for 15–20 minutes. Serve with salad or vegetables.

VEAL

CRUSTY ROAST VEAL (photograph on page 56)

Serves 8

One serve contains	
Carbohydrate	8 g
Calories	454
Kilojoules	1900

2 kg (4 lb) nut of veal
45 g (1½ oz) butter
1 onion, finely chopped
1 cup (8 fl oz) dry white wine
1 cup (8 fl oz) beef stock
salt
freshly ground black pepper
1 cup (4 oz) grated Gruyèye cheese
½ cup (2 oz) dry breadcrumbs

Preheat the oven to 180°C (350°F/Gas 4). Heat the butter in a frying pan and sauté the onion until soft. Remove the pan from the heat and add the grated cheese and breadcrumbs. Press the mixture over the veal (if it doesn't stick, first dampen the veal with a little white wine). Place the veal in a baking dish and pour the wine and stock around it (not over it). Bake, uncovered, for 2–2½ hours or until the veal is cooked. Baste occasionally. Serve with a crisp green salad.

HERBED SHOULDER OF VEAL

Fresh herbs enhance the flavour of the veal. They are easy to grow in your garden or in a pot on the window-sill.

Serves 8

One serve contains	
Carbohydrate	17 g
Calories	396
Kilojoules	1660

1 boned shoulder of veal
1 cup (8 fl oz) beef stock
salt
freshly ground black pepper
30 g (1 oz) butter

Stuffing

3 cups (6 oz) fresh breadcrumbs
1 small onion, finely chopped
1 egg, beaten
1 teaspoon dried mixed herbs (or 2 tablespoons fresh herbs)
1 tablespoon chopped parsley
salt and pepper

Preheat the oven to 180°C (350°F/Gas 4). Weigh the shoulder of veal and calculate the cooking time, allowing 30 minutes per 500 g (1 lb).

Stuffing: Combine all ingredients in a bowl. Mix thoroughly.

Fill the shoulder with the herb stuffing; tie firmly into shape. Place in a baking dish. Pour over the stock, sprinkle with salt and pepper and dot with butter. Place in pre-heated oven and baste frequently during cooking. Allow to stand for 15 minutes in a warm place before carving.

OSSO BUCCO

Serves 4

One serve contains	
Carbohydrate	10 g
Calories	306
Kilojoules	1280

4 slices veal foreshank
2 tablespoons flour
1 teaspoon salt
freshly ground black pepper
2 tablespoons oil
1 medium onion, chopped
1 clove garlic, crushed
1 carrot, diced
¾ cup (6 fl oz) dry white wine
1 cup (8 fl oz) beef stock
3 tablespoons tomato paste
¼ teaspoon ground thyme
bouquet garni
parsley sprigs for garnish

Secure the meat into round shapes with cotton. Coat the meat in the flour seasoned with salt and pepper. Heat the oil in a flameproof casserole or large saucepan. Brown the meat and set aside.

Sauté the onion, garlic and carrot until the onion is transparent. Add the wine and allow to boil for 1 minute. Stir in the remaining ingredients and return the meat to the pan; cover and simmer gently for 1½ hours. Turn meat occasionally to prevent it from drying out. Remove cotton from meat and lift out bouquet garni. Serve on a bed of rice and garnish with sprigs of parsley.

VEAL WITH APRICOTS

Serves 6

One serve contains	
Carbohydrate	19 g
Calories	370
Kilojoules	1550

1 tablespoon oil
6 veal steaks, lightly pounded
1 small onion, sliced
2 cloves garlic, crushed
1 green pepper, cut into strips
1 red pepper, cut into strips
2.5 cm (1 in) piece fresh root ginger, grated
pinch saffron
½ teaspoon cumin
½ teaspoon coriander
salt
pepper
125 g (4 oz) dried apricots, soaked in water then drained and chopped
30 g (1 oz) butter
1 tablespoon flour
¼ cup (2 fl oz) orange juice

Heat the oil in a flameproof casserole. Brown the veal on both sides. Add the onion, garlic, peppers, ginger, saffron, cumin, coriander, salt and pepper. Then add enough hot water to almost cover the meat. Cover and simmer gently for 1 hour, stirring occasionally. Add the chopped apricots and cook 15 minutes longer. Lift out veal and remove to a serving dish. Using a slotted spoon lift out the vegetables and apricots and keep warm in a separate dish. Bring the sauce to the boil and boil rapidly until slightly reduced. Strain.

Melt the butter in a clean saucepan; stir in the flour and cook for 1 minute. Remove from heat and stir in strained sauce. Return to heat and cook for 3–4 minutes, then add the orange juice. Pour the sauce over the veal, then scatter the meat with the cooked vegetables and apricots. Serve immediately with steamed vegetables or salad.

VEAL IN MUSHROOM SAUCE

We suggest you serve this dish with vegetable pasta. The colourful noodles are made from tomato, onion, spinach, corn and celery.

Serves 4

One serve contains	
Carbohydrate	6 g
Calories	299
Kilojoules	1250

500 g (1 lb) veal steak
1 tablespoon flour
1 teaspoon salt
freshly ground black pepper
1 tablespoon oil
1 small onion, chopped
1 clove garlic, crushed
250 g (8 oz) mushrooms, trimmed and quartered
½ cup (4 fl oz) dry white wine
1 tablespoon tomato paste
2 tablespoons sour cream
1 tablespoon chopped parsley

Cut veal into serving-size pieces. Coat the veal with flour seasoned with salt and pepper. Heat the oil in a heavy-based frying pan with a lid. Brown the veal, then remove and set aside.

Sauté the onion and garlic in the pan until soft. Add the mushrooms and cook for 2 minutes longer. Return the veal to the pan and add the wine and tomato paste. Cover and simmer for 30 minutes or until the veal is tender. Stir in the cream and reheat but do not boil. Sprinkle with the chopped parsley and serve immediately. Serve with vegetable noodles and salad.

SALTIMBOCCA

Prosciutto (raw Parma ham) gives additional flavour to the veal. If unavailable, thinly sliced ham is a suitable substitute.

Serves 4

One serve contains	
Carbohydrate	neg.
Calories	368
Kilojoules	1540

500 g (1 lb) veal steaks cut thinly and flattened with a meat mallet
125 g (4 oz) sliced prosciutto
fresh sage leaves or ½ teaspoon dried sage
1 tablespoon butter
¼ cup (2 fl oz) white wine
¼ cup (2 fl oz) beef stock
salt
freshly ground black pepper
sage leaves or parsley for garnish

Place a slice of prosciutto, cut the same size as the veal, on each piece of steak. Top with a sage leaf or a light sprinkling of dried sage. Roll up and fasten with toothpicks.

Heat the butter in a heavy-based frying pan. Brown the rolls on all sides. Reduce the heat and add the wine, stock, salt and pepper. Stir to lift the sediment in the pan. Cover and simmer gently for 20–25 minutes or until tender and the liquid has slightly thickened. Remove the toothpicks and serve immediately. Serve with brown rice and salad.

VEAL STRIPS IN HERBED SAUCE

Serves 6

One serve contains	
Carbohydrate	9 g
Calories	430
Kilojoules	1800

1 kg (2 lb) thin veal steaks
⅓ cup (1½ oz) flour
1½ teaspoons salt
freshly ground black pepper
60 g (2 oz) butter
¾ cup (6 fl oz) dry white wine
1 teaspoon basil
3 teaspoons chopped parsley
1½ cups (12 fl oz) natural non-fat yoghurt
1 large egg yolk
chopped fresh herbs for garnish

Cut veal into thin strips. Combine the flour, salt and a generous grind of black pepper in a plastic bag. Add the veal strips, shake to coat veal. Shake off any excess flour. Heat the butter in a flameproof casserole. Brown the veal on all sides (divide into 2 or 3 lots). Add the wine, basil and parsley. Bring to the boil then cover and simmer for 20 minutes or until tender.

Combine the yoghurt and egg yolk. Remove the casserole from heat, add the yoghurt mixture. Re-heat but do not boil. Garnish with fresh herbs and serve with wholemeal noodles and green vegetables.

VEAL CARBONNADE

Serves 6

One serve contains	
Carbohydrate	23 g
Calories	448
Kilojoules	1875

3 tablespoons oil
4 medium potatoes, diced
3 medium carrots, sliced
3 medium onions, chopped
2 sticks celery, chopped
750 g (1½ lb) stewing veal, cubed
salt
freshly ground black pepper
3 cups (24 fl oz) beer
½ cup (4 fl oz) reduced cream
parsley for garnish

Heat the oil in a flameproof casserole. Sauté the vegetables until golden brown. Remove from casserole and set aside. Add the veal to the pan and brown on all sides. Return vegetables to the pan and season with salt and pepper.

Add the beer, cover and simmer gently for 30–40 minutes or until the veal is tender. Remove from heat and stir in the cream. Re-heat, but do not boil. Sprinkle with parsley and serve immediately with brown rice and green vegetables.

VEAL WITH ARTICHOKES

Serves 4

One serve contains	
Carbohydrate	13 g
Calories	400
Kilojoules	1675

500 g (1 lb) stewing steak, cut into 2.5 cm (1 in) cubes
¼ teaspoon salt
½ teaspoon freshly ground black pepper
½ teaspoon oregano
1 tablespoon oil
1 large onion, chopped
4 fresh or canned artichoke hearts, cut into thick slices
½ cup (4 fl oz) chicken stock
½ cup (4 fl oz) dry white wine
2 teaspoons cornflour (cornstarch)
chopped parsley for garnish

Preheat the oven to 180°C (350°F/Gas 4). Combine the veal, salt, pepper and oregano in a plastic bag. Shake over the veal until it is evenly coated. Set aside.

Heat the oil in a frying pan. Sauté the onion until golden. Remove to a flameproof casserole. Add the veal to the pan and brown on all sides (cook in 2–3 lots). Transfer to casserole dish.

Add the artichoke hearts to the pan and brown on both sides. Place on top of the veal. Pour the stock and wine into the pan, bring to the boil, stirring to lift sediment in the pan. Pour over the casserole.

Cover and bake for 1 hour or until the veal is tender. Thicken with the cornflour blended with a little cold water. Bring to the boil and serve immediately garnished with the chopped parsley.

LAMB

SOUVLAKIA

A popular Greek dish of skewered lamb that is marinated overnight before cooking.

Serves 4

One serve contains	
Carbohydrate	2 g
Calories	272
Kilojoules	1140

750 g (1½ lb) boneless leg of lamb, trimmed
1 medium onion, cut into quarters and layers separated
2 cloves garlic, crushed
½ cup (4 fl oz) dry white wine
3 bay leaves, broken into quarters
½ teaspoon dried marjoram
1½ teaspoons salt
freshly ground black pepper

Cut meat into 2.5 cm (1 in) squares. Place in a large glass bowl. Combine all the remaining ingredients and pour over the meat. Mix well. Cover and marinate overnight in the refrigerator (turn meat occasionally).

To cook, thread the meat on to four skewers, placing the pieces of onion and bay leaves between the cubes of lamb. Cook the skewered lamb under a hot griller (broiler) for 15–20 minutes, turning and brushing frequently with the marinade. Serve with steamed rice and a selection of salads.

ROAST LAMB WITH PORT

Serves 8

One serve contains	
Carbohydrate	20 g
Calories	659
Kilojoules	2760

Apple Stuffing

30 g (1 oz) butter
1 medium apple, diced
2 slices bacon, chopped
1 medium onion, chopped
1 clove garlic, crushed
2 cups (4 oz) fresh breadcrumbs
2 tablespoons chopped parsley
1 egg, lightly beaten
salt
freshly ground black pepper

Roast

2 kg (4 lb) shoulder lamb, boned
30 g (1 oz) butter
½ cup (4 fl oz) port
2 tablespoons tomato sauce
1 tablespoon vinegar
½ teaspoon Worcestershire sauce
2 tablespoons flour
2½ cups (20 fl oz) water
2 tablespoons chopped fresh mint
salt
freshly ground black pepper

Apple Stuffing: Heat the butter in a frying pan. Gently sauté the apple, bacon, onion and garlic for 3–4 minutes. Remove from heat and add remaining ingredients. Mix well.

Preheat the oven to 190°C (375°F/Gas 5). Spread lamb out on a board, skin side down. Press apple stuffing over the meat, finishing 2.5 cm (1 in) from edges. Roll up tightly, tie with string at 2.5 cm (1 in) intervals. Place in a baking dish and dot with butter. Bake for 30 minutes, reduce heat to 180°C (350°F/Gas 4) and cook for 30 minutes longer. Mix half of the port with the tomato sauce, vinegar and Worcestershire sauce. Pour over lamb and bake for another 30 minutes or until tender. Baste frequently.

Remove lamb from dish, keep warm while making sauce. Place baking dish over high heat, evaporate most of the liquid. Remove the pan from heat and stir in the flour. Add water. Return to heat and stir until the sauce thickens. Reduce heat, add the mint, remaining port and season with salt and pepper. Pour some of the sauce over the lamb and serve the remainder in a gravyboat.

CREOLE CHOPS

Serves 4

One serve contains	
Carbohydrate	5 g
Calories	299
Kilojoules	1250

8 lamb chops, trimmed
1 medium onion, roughly chopped
1 clove garlic, crushed
1 red or green pepper, seeded and chopped
1 large tomato, skinned and chopped
1 tablespoon tomato sauce
¼ teaspoon basil
1 teaspoon salt
freshly ground black pepper

Cook the chops in a heavy frying pan. Remove to a hot serving dish. Cover, keeping them warm while making the sauce.

Reduce heat of frying pan, sauté the onion until soft. Add the garlic and pepper, cook for a further 2 minutes. Stir in the tomato, tomato sauce, basil, salt and pepper. Cover and simmer for 5 minutes. Pour the sauce over the chops and serve immediately. Serve with new potatoes and crisp green vegetables.

CHUMP CHOPS WITH CHICKEN LIVERS (photograph on page 58)

Serves 6

One serve contains	
Carbohydrate	3 g
Calories	203
Kilojoules	850

6 thick chump chops
45 g (1½ oz) butter or margarine
155 g (5 oz) chicken livers
1 onion, chopped
1 tablespoon lemon juice
½ teaspoon curry powder
1 teaspoon salt
freshly ground black pepper
90 g (3 oz) button mushrooms, sliced
1 teaspoon chopped parsley

Trim excess fat from chops. Slit a pocket in each chop and set aside. Heat 30 g of the butter in a frying pan. When bubbly, add the livers and onion; sauté until soft. Remove and mash to a smooth paste. Add the lemon juice, curry powder, salt and pepper. Spoon stuffing into chops. Cook under a pre-heated griller (broiler).

Meanwhile, heat the remaining butter in a frying pan. Sauté the mushrooms, then add the parsley and garnish the chops with them before serving. Serve with butter beans, carrots, asparagus and grilled tomato.

CASSEROLED LAMB CHOPS

Serves 6

One serve contains	
Carbohydrate	19 g
Calories	380
Kilojoules	1590

1 kg (2 lb) lamb forequarter chops
¼ cup (1 oz) flour
1 teaspoon salt
freshly ground black pepper
2 tablespoons oil
1 large onion, sliced
440 g (14 oz) canned tomato soup
1 cup (8 fl oz) water
3 medium carrots, peeled and cut in half
½ cup (2 oz) fresh or frozen green peas

Trim fat from chops and coat with seasoned flour. Reserve any excess flour. Heat the oil in a large saucepan or a frying pan with a lid. Brown the chops on both sides. Set aside.

Add the onion, cook for a few minutes. Remove pan from the heat and stir in the remaining seasoned flour. Return to heat and cook for 1 minute. Add the tomato soup, water and carrots; return chops to the liquid. Cover and cook over a gentle heat for 2 hours. Stir in the peas 15–20 minutes before end of cooking. Serve with mashed potatoes and green vegetables.

STUFFED AUBERGINE

Eggplant with a typically Middle Eastern flavour from its main ingredients: lamb, rice, tomato and mint.

Serves 4

One serve contains	
Carbohydrate	16 g
Calories	382
Kilojoules	1600

2 eggplants (aubergines)
salt
1 tablespoon oil

Filling

1 tablespoon oil
1 medium onion, finely chopped
500 g (1 lb) lean minced lamb
2 tablespoons tomato paste
1½ cups (7½ oz) cooked brown rice
2 tablespoons chopped mint
1 teaspoon salt
freshly ground black pepper
mint or parsley for garnish

Preheat the oven to 180°C (350°F/Gas 4). Cut the eggplants in half lengthwise. With a sharp knife, make criss-cross incisions in the flesh. Sprinkle with salt and allow to stand for 30 minutes. Wash and pat dry with paper towels. Scoop out the flesh, leaving 1 cm (½ in) in the shell. Lightly brush the shells with oil. Chop the flesh into 1 cm (½ in) pieces.

Filling: Heat the oil in a large saucepan or frying pan. Sauté the onions until soft. Add the eggplant flesh and cook for another minute. Add the minced lamb and cook until browned. Stir in the tomato paste, rice and mint. Season with salt and pepper.

Spoon filling into each eggplant half. Place in a greased baking dish with ½ cup water in the base. Cover with foil and bake for 25–30 minutes. Serve hot or cold, garnished with mint or parsley.

LAMB CHOPS PAPRIKA

Serves 4

One serve contains	
Carbohydrate	6 g
Calories	179
Kilojoules	750

4 thick chump chops
2 teaspoons oil
2 medium onions, thinly sliced
1 clove garlic, crushed
3 teaspoons paprika
1 tablespoon flour
2 cups (16 fl oz) chicken stock
1 tablespoon tomato paste
bay leaf
1 teaspoon salt
freshly ground black pepper
90 g (3 oz) non-fat natural yoghurt
parsley for garnish

Trim excess fat from chops. Heat a frying pan with a lid. Brown the chops on both sides. Remove and set aside.

Heat the oil in the pan and sauté the onions until soft. Add the garlic and paprika and cook for 1–2 minutes. Stir in the flour and cook for another minute. Add the stock all at once, stirring to combine. Then add the bay leaf, salt and pepper.

Return the chops to the pan, cover and simmer for 45–55 minutes or until the chops are tender. Place chops on a serving dish, spoon over sauce then top with yoghurt. Garnish with parsley and serve with wholemeal or vegetable noodles.

PORK

ROAST PORK WITH APRICOTS (photograph opposite)

Serves 8

One serve contains	
Carbohydrate	9 g
Calories	380
Kilojoules	1590

1 x 1.5 kg (3 lb) pork neck (or loin of pork with fat removed)
100 g (3½ oz) dried apricots, soaked in water until soft, then drained
2 slices lean bacon

Preheat the oven to 180°C (350°F/Gas 4). Cut a large pocket in the side of the pork. Fill with the apricots and 1 slice of chopped bacon. Seal the opening with a skewer or sew up with needle and thread. Place the remaining slice of bacon on the top and place in a baking dish.

Cover and bake for 1½ hours or until cooked. In the last 30 minutes of cooking, remove cover and increase the temperature to crisp the top. Serve with jacket potatoes and steamed vegetables.

PORK FILLETS IN SOY SAUCE

Serves 4

One serve contains	
Carbohydrate	4 g
Calories	296
Kilojoules	1240

500 g (1 lb) pork fillets
(or 4 pork chops if unavailable)
1 tablespoon soy sauce
1 tablespoon dry sherry
1 teaspoon salt
½ teaspoon freshly ground black pepper
1 tablespoon cornflour (cornstarch)
1 tablespoon oil

Sauce
1 tablespoon oil
1 small onion, chopped
½ cup (4 fl oz) dry white wine
¼ cup (2 fl oz) chicken stock
1 tablespoon soy sauce
2 teaspoons cornflour (cornstarch)

Sprinkle the pork fillets with the soy sauce and sherry. Rub in the salt and pepper. Dust with the cornflour and set aside. Heat the oil in a large frying pan. Add the pork and stir-fry on high heat for 2 minutes then reduce heat and cook 4–5 minutes longer or until tender. If using chops, pan-fry until cooked for about 20 minutes (depending on size of chops).

Sauce: Heat the oil in a small saucepan. Sauté the onion until soft but not brown. Pour in the wine, stock and soy sauce and boil for 1 minute. Add the cornflour blended with a little cold water, and cook, stirring frequently for 1 minute or until the sauce thickens. Pour the sauce over the pork then transfer to a serving dish. Serve immediately with brown rice and a cucumber salad.

Roast Pork with Apricots (page 92)

Orange Marigold (page 98)

SAGE FILLETS WITH MUSTARD SAUCE

Fillets of pork flavoured with sage and served in a mustard cream sauce.

Serves 4

One serve contains	
Carbohydrate	1 g
Calories	534
Kilojoules	2235

750 g (1½ lb) pork fillets
½ teaspoon salt
½ teaspoon freshly ground black pepper
30 g (1 oz) butter
3 teaspoons ground sage
¼ cup (2 fl oz) dry white wine
125 g (4 oz) Emmenthal cheese, cut into slices
2 teaspoons prepared French mustard
⅓ cup (2½ fl oz) cream

Rub the fillets all over with the salt and pepper. Heat the butter in a large flameproof casserole. When the foam subsides, add the pork fillets and sprinkle the sage on them. Brown the meat on all sides for about 6–8 minutes. Add the wine, cook for 1 minute. Reduce the heat, cover and simmer for 30 minutes or until cooked. Turn the meat occasionally.

Remove the casserole from the heat and transfer the fillets to a chopping board. Make 2–3 deep incisions along each fillet. Spread the cheese slices with the mustard and place a slice in each incision. Return to the casserole, cook for 5–10 minutes or until the cheese has melted. Transfer the pork fillets to a warmed serving dish. Add the cream to the pan juices, heat but do not boil. Pour the cream sauce over the fillets and serve immediately. Serve with new potatoes and salad.

PORK CHOPS CHARCUTIÈRE

Serves 4

One serve contains	
Carbohydrate	2 g
Calories	217
Kilojoules	910

4 pork chops
2 teaspoons oil
½ teaspoon salt
freshly ground black pepper
½ cup (1 oz) spring onions (scallions), chopped
½ cup (4 fl oz) dry white wine
2 tablespoons vinegar
1 cup (8 fl oz) beef stock
1 tablespoon tomato paste
bouquet garni
3 teaspoons French or English mustard
⅓ cup (2 oz) sliced gherkins

Trim the fat from the chops. Heat the oil in a frying pan. Cook the chops, turning once, for about 20–25 minutes. Remove from the pan, sprinkle with the salt and pepper, cover and keep warm while making the sauce.

Add spring onions to the pan, sauté for 1 minute. Pour in the wine and vinegar, stirring to lift the brown sediment in the pan. Boil until reduced by half. Reduce the heat, add the stock, tomato paste and bouquet garni. Simmer for 10 minutes, stirring occasionally. Remove the bouquet garni and stir in the mustard and gherkins. Add the chops and heat through before serving. Serve with jacket potatoes and steamed vegetables.

PORK CHOPS WITH PEACH SAUCE

Serves 4

One serve contains	
Carbohydrate	10 g
Calories	230
Kilojoules	965

4 lean pork chops
freshly ground black pepper
1 tablespoon oil
6 unsweetened peach halves
1¼ cups (10 fl oz) peach fruit juice (from the canned peaches)
3 whole black peppercorns
1 tablespoon white vinegar
cinnamon
3 teaspoons cornflour (cornstarch)
parsley sprigs for garnish

Trim excess fat from the pork. Sprinkle both sides with ground pepper. Heat the oil, brown the chops on both sides, then reduce the heat and cook for 20 minutes, turning occasionally. Remove the chops to a serving dish and keep warm. Meanwhile, mash or purée the peaches. Combine the purée, juice, peppercorns, vinegar and cinnamon in a saucepan. Bring to the boil and simmer gently for 8–10 minutes.

Stir in the cornflour blended with a little cold water. Bring to the boil and simmer for 1 minute or until the sauce thickens. Pour the sauce over the chops, garnish with parsley and serve immediately.

TRANSYLVANIAN SAUERKRAUT

Traditionally served with a tossed salad and black bread.

Serves 8

One serve contains	
Carbohydrate	15 g
Calories	465
Kilojoules	1945

1 tablespoon oil
1 medium onion, chopped
500 g (1 lb) cubed pork
1 teaspoon paprika
½ teaspoon salt
freshly ground black pepper
625 g (20 oz) canned sauerkraut
250 g (8 oz) Polish sausage, chopped
125 g (4 oz) lean bacon, diced
1½ cups cooked rice (½ cup raw)
250 g (8 oz) light sour cream

Preheat the oven to 200°C (400°F/Gas 6). Heat the oil in a frying pan with a lid. Sauté the onion and pork. Add paprika, salt and pepper. Cover, cook gently for 10–15 minutes.

Place a layer of sauerkraut in the base of a casserole dish. The subsequent layers should be of cooked rice, pork, sour cream, rice, sausages, bacon and sour cream. Finish with sauerkraut and sour cream. Bake for 20 minutes and serve immediately.

DESSERTS

Few desserts are as elegant as fruit. The jewel colours and natural shapes of fruit provide a delightful simplicity. Yoghurt is the perfect instant sauce complementing all kinds of fruit and makes a flavourful and low-kilojoule substitute in recipes that normally call for sour cream or cream. Yoghurt and buttermilk, which are both cultured milk products, give desserts a surprisingly delightful twist.

With the majority of people 'thinking slim', sugar-free products are no longer hard to find. Special diet products are now scattered throughout the many shelves of the supermarket. Let your imagination take over and experiment with your traditional family favourites! You will always have a backstop with our well-tested recipes.

By using fruit to naturally sweeten your desserts, you reduce the artificial sweetener needed and so minimise any bitter after-taste.

One of the many wonderful things about desserts is that there is always one to meet any occasion, any weather, any person or any budget.

CREAMED RICE

Serves 4

4 cups (1 litre) milk
½ cup (3 oz) rice
small piece lemon rind
½ teaspoon liquid artificial sweetener
½ teaspoon vanilla essence

One serve contains	
Carbohydrate	30 g
Calories	245
Kilojoules	1025

Place the milk, rice and lemon rind in the top of a double boiler. Cook until the rice is tender, for about 1 hour, stirring occasionally.

Add the sweetener and vanilla essence. Remove the lemon rind.

Variation: Add 1½ tablespoons of raisins or sultanas in the last 10 minutes of cooking.

APPLE AMBROSIA

Food of the gods!

Serves 6

4 medium cooking apples
¼ cup (1 oz) raisins
¼ cup (1 oz) roughly chopped walnuts
300 g (9½ oz) natural yoghurt
¼ teaspoon cinnamon

One serve contains	
Carbohydrate	20 g
Calories	117
Kilojoules	490

Peel, core and thinly slice apples. Cook very gently in a small amount of water. Drain. Mix all of the ingredients together.

Spoon the mixture into parfait glasses and sprinkle with extra cinnamon. Chill before serving. Top with extra yoghurt if desired.

BANANA CREAM

Serves 6

One serve contains	
Carbohydrate	22 g
Calories	129
Kilojoules	540

2½ tablespoons custard powder
2 cups (16 fl oz) milk
½ teaspoon vanilla essence
85 g (3 oz) packet diabetic lemon jelly crystals
5 medium bananas
2 tablespoons fresh orange juice
¼ teaspoon liquid artificial sweetener (optional)

Blend the custard powder with a little of the milk. Place remaining milk in a saucepan. Bring to the boil and add the blended custard powder. Stir until the custard thickens. Add the vanilla essence. Chill.

Make the jelly according to directions on the packet. Pour into a large mixing bowl, refrigerate until partially set. Mash the bananas, add to the jelly with the custard and orange juice. Beat until light and fluffy. Gradually add sweetener if desired. Pour into a large serving dish and refrigerate until set.

ORANGE MARIGOLD (photograph on page 94)

Even desserts can boost protein counts! Ricotta is a fresh cheese made from milk protein.

Serves 6

One serve contains	
Carbohydrate	24 g
Calories	240
Kilojoules	1005

2 oranges
1 tablespoon Kirsch
375 g (12 oz) ricotta cheese
¾ cup (3 oz) ground almonds
3 teaspoons finely grated orange rind
2 teaspoons orange juice
½ teaspoon vanilla essence
⅓ cup (2 oz) raisins
⅓ cup (2 oz) sultanas
toasted slivered almonds for decoration

Peel the oranges, removing all outside pith. Cut into thin even slices and place around the base and sides of a mould or pie dish. Sprinkle with Kirsch.

Mix together the remaining ingredients. Add a little artificial sweetener if desired. Spoon the mixture carefully into the prepared mould. Level off the top. Chill. When firmly set, unmould on to a serving dish and decorate with toasted slivered almonds.

SUMMER YOGHURT CUP

Try this delicious combination or experiment with any fruit of your choice. Sweeten if necessary, but we like the sharp flavour of the yoghurt.

Serves 4

One serve contains	
Carbohydrate	34 g
Calories	168
Kilojoules	705

500 g (1 lb) non-fat natural yoghurt
pulp of 4 passionfruit
1 cup (10 oz) fresh or canned unsweetened
pineapple pieces, drained
2 bananas, diced

Combine all ingredients in a bowl, mix well. Spoon into individual parfait glasses and chill until serving time.

GRAPE DELIGHT

Serves 6

One serve contains	
Carbohydrate	24 g
Calories	139
Kilojoules	580

Ricotta Sauce
250 g (8 oz) ricotta cheese, crumbled
½ cup (4 fl oz) fresh orange juice
rind of 1 lemon
½ teaspoon cinnamon

Salad
1½ cups (8 oz) seedless white grapes
1½ cups (8 oz) black grapes, halved and seeded
1 large banana, sliced
pulp of 2 passionfruit
1 Kiwi fruit (Chinese gooseberry), sliced

Combine ricotta cheese, orange juice, lemon rind and cinnamon in a blender or processor. Blend until smooth.

Mix the grapes, banana and passionfruit together, stir in the ricotta sauce. Spoon into a glass dish and decorate with the sliced kiwi fruit.

PEARS POACHED IN WHITE WINE

I prefer this without sweetener, so taste before adding. The flavour improves if the pears are left in the syrup overnight.

Serves 6

One serve contains	
Carbohydrate	22 g
Calories	85
Kilojoules	355

6 medium pears
2½ cups (20 fl oz) dry white wine
2½ cups (20 fl oz) water
1 teaspoon grated lemon rind
1 tablespoon lemon juice
5 cm (2 in) cinnamon stick
4 whole cloves
liquid artificial sweetener (optional)

Peel the pears thinly, leaving the stalks in place and keeping a good pear shape. Place the pears in a medium-sized saucepan. Add all the other ingredients. The liquid should just cover the pears (if necessary add a little extra wine and water). Cover and simmer gently for 20–30 minutes or until cooked.

Remove pears to a glass or plastic container. Strain liquid over the pears. Check sweetness and add liquid artificial sweetener if desired. Cover and refrigerate until quite cold. Serve pears in individual dishes with the sauce spooned over.

APPLE SNOW

Serves 6

One serve contains	
Carbohydrate	9 g
Calories	41
Kilojoules	170

3 teaspoons gelatine
¼ cup hot water
2 cups (14 oz) unsweetened pie apple
¼ cup (2 fl oz) lemon juice
½–1 teaspoon cinnamon
½ teaspoon liquid artificial sweetener (optional)
whites of 3 large eggs

Dissolve the gelatine in hot water. Allow to cool. Purée or sieve apples into a large bowl. Add the dissolved gelatine, lemon juice, cinnamon and sweetener, if desired.

Beat the egg whites until stiff peaks form, fold into apple mixture. Pour into a serving bowl and refrigerate until set.

PINEAPPLE BREEZE

Simple, but delicious.

Serves 6

One serve contains	
Carbohydrate	13 g
Calories	86
Kilojoules	360

440 g (14 oz) canned unsweetened pineapple, crushed
1 packet diabetic lemon jelly crystals
410 g (13 oz) evaporated skim milk, well chilled
2 tablespoons lemon juice

Bring the pineapple to the boil. Remove from the heat and add the jelly crystals. Stir until dissolved. Chill the mixture until nearly set.

Beat together the pineapple jelly, evaporated milk and lemon juice until light and fluffy. Pour into serving dish and refrigerate until set.

SKEWERED FRUIT MEDLEY

Any firm fruit in season can be used for the kebabs. Try strawberries, grapes, peaches or rockmelon.

Serves 4

One serve contains	
Carbohydrate	36 g
Calories	145
Kilojoules	605

2 medium oranges
3 bananas
2 red apples
¼ cup (2 fl oz) concentrated orange juice
2 teaspoons kirsch
½ teaspoon ground ginger
1 teaspoon lemon juice
liquid artificial sweetener (optional)

Peel and cut oranges and bananas into chunks. Core the apples and cut into large pieces, leaving the skin on. Thread the fruit alternately on to four skewers. Combine remaining ingredients in a jug.

Cook the kebabs under a hot grill or over a barbecue, basting frequently with the orange sauce. Cook for 10–15 minutes or until light golden.

BUTTERMILK SHIMMY

Serves 6

One serve contains	
Carbohydrate	7 g
Calories	46
Kilojoules	195

½ cup (4 fl oz) fruit juice (drained from canned fruit)
½ cup (4 fl oz) water
1 packet raspberry of strawberry diabetic jelly crystals
1½ cups (12 fl oz) buttermilk, well chilled
1 cup (8 oz) canned unsweetened fruit, drained and chopped (try peaches, pears or fruit salad)

Combine the fruit juice and water in a saucepan. Bring to the boil and add jelly crystals. Stir to dissolve. Pour into a large bowl, and refrigerate until nearly set.

Using an electric mixer, beat the jelly with the buttermilk until it doubles in volume and becomes light and fluffy. Fold in chopped fruit and pour into a serving bowl. Refrigerate until set.

Variations

Fruit Smoothie: Combine the partially set jelly and remaining ingredients in a blender jar, blend until smooth. Refrigerate until set.

Shimmy Parfait: Prepare the whip as above, omitting the fruit. Serve in parfait glasses in layers alternating with the fruit. Top with chopped nuts or toasted coconut.

TROPICAL ISLANDER PIE

A blend of tropical flavours — compliments will flow!

Serves 8

One serve contains	
Carbohydrate	12 g
Calories	108
Kilojoules	455

1 baked wholemeal pastry crust (see page 114)
400 g (13 oz) ricotta cheese
⅓ cup (2½ fl oz) evaporated skim milk
2 bananas, mashed
pulp of 4 passionfruits
3 tablespoons lemon juice
extra passionfruit for topping

Beat the ricotta cheese and evaporated milk until smooth. Stir in the mashed banana, passionfruit pulp and lemon juice.

Pour into the pie crust and refrigerate until set. Top with the extra passionfruit pulp before serving.

CONFETTI CREAM CAKE

A dazzling party attraction.

Serves 10

One serve contains	
Carbohydrate	2 g
Calories	215
Kilojoules	900

1 each of diabetic orange, lime and strawberry jellies
90 g (3 oz) walnuts
1 cup (8 fl oz) boiling water
1 packet diabetic lemon jelly crystals
250 g (8 oz) cream cheese at room temperature
2 teaspoons liquid artificial sweetener
1¼ cups (10 fl oz) thickened cream
whipped cream and lemon rind for decoration

Prepare orange, lime and strawberry jellies. Chop the walnuts until very fine. Sprinkle on to the bottom of a 23 cm (9 in) springform pan. Dissolve the lemon jelly crystals in the boiling water. Chill until nearly set.

In a large bowl, beat the cream cheese until smooth. Add sweetener and partially set jelly. Beat until light and fluffy. Whip the cream until doubled in volume, fold into the cream cheese mixture.

Cut the prepared jellies into small cubes. Using a spatula, gently stir into the cream mixture and pour into the prepared springform pan. Chill until set. Before serving, remove the sides from the springform pan. Pile the extra whipped cream in the centre and top with twists of lemon rind.

PRUNE WHIP

Serves 8

One serve contains	
Carbohydrate	17 g
Calories	72
Kilojoules	300

1 tablespoon gelatine
1½ cups (12 fl oz) boiling water
200 g (6½ oz) pitted dried prunes
3 teaspoons lemon juice
1 teaspoon liquid artificial sweetener
5 egg whites

Dissolve the gelatine in boiling water. Cool. Purée or sieve the prunes, add to the dissolved gelatine with the lemon juice and sweetener. Refrigerate until nearly set.

Using an electric mixer whip the prune mixture until light and fluffy. Beat the egg whites until stiff and lightly fold into prune mixture. Pour into a large glass serving bowl and refrigerate until set.

PEACH RATAFIA

These sliced peaches in a liqueur-flavoured strawberry sauce are very simple to make.

Serves 6

One serve contains	
Carbohydrate	20 g
Calories	94
Kilojoules	395

6 fresh peaches
500 g (1 lb) fresh strawberries
1 tablespoon kirsch
liquid artificial sweetener (optional)
slivered almonds for decoration

Peel and slice the peaches into a glass serving bowl or individual dishes.

Purée or mash the strawberries. Just before serving add the liqueur and sweetener if desired (depending on the ripeness of the strawberries). Pour over the sliced peaches and serve decorated with slivered almonds.

BAKED CUSTARD

Serves 6

One serve contains	
Carbohydrate	6 g
Calories	134
Kilojoules	560

3 cups (24 fl oz) milk
4 eggs
1 teaspoon vanilla essence
1 teaspoon liquid artificial sweetener
grated nutmeg

Preheat the oven to 150°C (300°F/Gas 2). Beat together the milk, eggs, vanilla and sweetener. Pour into a greased ovenproof dish. Stand the dish in a tray of hot water and sprinkle with grated nutmeg.

Bake for 40 minutes or until set. Remove the dish immediately from the hot water to prevent further cooking.

PINEAPPLE CHEESECAKE

Serves 8

One serve contains	
Carbohydrate	26 g
Calories	244
Kilojoules	1020

Base

210 g (7 oz) wheatmeal biscuit crumbs
75 g (2½ oz) melted butter
¼ teaspoon cinnamon

Filling

440 g (14 oz) canned unsweetened pineapple, crushed
3 teaspoons gelatine
3 eggs
200 g (6½ oz) cottage cheese
artificial liquid sweetener (optional)

Base: Mix the crumbs with melted butter and cinnamon. Press into the bottom of a spring-form tin. Chill.

Filling: Drain the pineapple and reserve liquid. Soften the gelatine in half of the drained pineapple juice, reserve remainder. Separate the eggs.

Combine the yolks and remaining pineapple juice in a double boiler. Cook over hot water stirring continually until thickened. Remove from heat and stir in the gelatine until dissolved.

Push the cottage cheese through a sieve or blend until smooth. Stir the pineapple and cottage cheese into the custard mixture. Beat egg whites until stiff peaks form, and fold into the mixture. Pour into the prepared base. Chill until set.

BOMBE ABRICOTINE

This is a very elegant dessert. Although this recipe uses canned apricots, you may substitute strawberries or mulberries. Bombe Abricotine may be accompanied by wafer biscuits.

Serves 16

One serve contains	
Carbohydrate	15 g
Calories	181
Kilojoules	760

8 cups (2 litres) vanilla ice cream, slightly softened in the refrigerator
4 egg yolks
liquid artificial sweetener to taste
2 tablespoons orange juice
¼ cup (2 fl oz) rum
425 g (13½ oz) canned pie apricots
1 cup (8 fl oz) thickened cream
hulled strawberries and toasted slivered almonds for decoration

Chill a glass bowl 2.5 cm (1 in) smaller than the mould. Prepare a chilled 8-cup (2 litre) bombe mould by wetting and then spooning a little of the ice cream into the base. Working quickly, so that the ice cream doesn't melt, spoon a few scoops of the ice cream into the mould. With the back of a metal spoon, pat the ice-cream firmly against the sides of the mould. Return the remaining ice cream to the freezer. Place the smaller bowl inside the mould, so that the ice cream forms a solid wall between the bowl and the mould. Freeze for 1 hour or until completely firm.

Meanwhile, prepare the filling. Beat together the egg yolks, sweetener, orange juice and rum. Mix in the pie apricots. Chill for 30 minutes. Whip the cream until doubled in volume and fold into the chilled apricot mixture.

Remove the bombe mould from the freezer and lift out the glass bowl. If the bowl sticks, pour a little hot water into the bowl and it should slide out easily. Spoon the apricot mixture into the centre of the bombe, filling almost to the top. Freeze for 2–3 hours or until the apricot filling is quite firm. Cut the remaining ice cream into slices and place on top of the apricot mixture. Smooth with a knife. Cover the mould with foil and freeze for 6–12 hours or until it feels firm to the touch.

Just before serving, place the serving plate in the freezer to chill thoroughly. Unmould the bombe by dipping the mould in hot water for 20–30 seconds. Put the plate upside down on top of the mould. Holding the plate and mould firmly, turn over quickly and the bombe should slip out smoothly. Decorate with the hulled strawberries and toasted almonds.

STRAWBERRY SOUFFLÉ

This one's not for weight-watchers.

Serves 6

One serve contains	
Carbohydrate	4 g
Calories	209
Kilojoules	875

3 teaspoons gelatine
⅓ cup hot water
250 g (8 oz) punnet strawberries, washed and hulled
1 tablespoon brandy
1 teaspoon liquid artificial sweetener
3 egg whites
1¼ cups (10 fl oz) thickened cream, whipped

Dissolve the gelatine in the hot water; allow to cool. Mash or purée the strawberries (slice and reserve a few for decoration). Place in a large bowl and add the brandy and sweetener. Stir the dissolved gelatine into the strawberry mixture; refrigerate until just beginning to set.

Whisk the egg whites until stiff; fold into the strawberry mixture with the whipped cream, being careful not to overmix. Check sweetness. Pour into a glass serving dish or individual parfait glasses. Refrigerate until set. Serve with sliced strawberries piled in the centre.

CLAFOUTI

A delicious thick fruit pancake. Any fruit can be used for this dessert. Try stoned cherries, grapes, apricots, berries or bananas.

Serves 6

One serve contains	
Carbohydrate	15 g
Calories	121
Kilojoules	505

2 large cooking apples, sliced
1 cup (8 fl oz) milk
3 eggs
½ cup (2 oz) sifted flour
2 teaspoons vanilla essence
¼ teaspoon liquid artificial sweetener

Preheat the oven to 180°C (350°F/Gas 4). Lightly grease a 20 cm (8 in) pie dish or shallow baking dish. Place apple slices in the base of dish.

Combine all remaining ingredients in a blender or processor. Blend until smooth. Pour batter over the apple and bake for 30–40 minutes or until set. Serve warm.

APPLE CRUMBLE

Serves 8

One serve contains	
Carbohydrate	16 g
Calories	93
Kilojoules	390

Apples

6 cooking apples, peeled and thinly sliced
½ cup (4 fl oz) water
2 tablespoons sultanas or raisins
½ teaspoon mixed spice

Crumble Topping

1½ tablespoons self-raising flour
3 tablespoons coconut
1 weetbix, crushed
½ teaspoon vanilla essence
½ teaspoon liquid artificial sweetener
20 g (⅔ oz) butter or margarine

Apples: Preheat the oven to 180°C (350°F/Gas 4). Combine the apples, water, sultanas and mixed spice in a saucepan. Simmer gently over a low heat until just tender. Pour into an ovenproof dish.
Crumble Topping: Mix together flour, coconut, weetbix, vanilla and sweetener. Rub in the butter until the mixture resembles breadcrumbs. Sprinkle the topping over the apples and bake for 20 minutes.

Variation

Substitute ⅓ cup (½ oz) crushed cornflakes for the weetbix. Add 1 teaspoon of skim milk powder.

PÊCHES AMANDES

Serves 6

One serve contains	
Carbohydrate	13 g
Calories	158
Kilojoules	660

12 canned unsweetened peach halves
½ cup (4 fl oz) dry sherry
125 g (4 oz) toasted almonds, slivered

Cut some foil into 6 rectangles. Place two peach halves on each piece of foil. Fold up the sides of the foil and pour 1 tablespoon sherry over each serving.

Seal foil firmly and cook on the barbecue for 5–10 minutes or until hot. To serve, remove peaches to individual glass dishes and sprinkle with toasted almonds. Serve with ice cream.

PEACH TRIFLE

If you prefer your trifle without sherry, sprinkle the cake with peach juice instead.

Serves 6

One serve contains	
Carbohydrate	28 g
Calories	333
Kilojoules	1395

2½ cups (20 fl oz) thick custard
½ quantity Basic Buttercake recipe (see page 107) or stale sponge cake
3 tablespoons dry sherry
2 fresh or canned unsweetened peaches, sliced
1 prepared diabetic jelly, refrigerated until set
⅓ cup (2½ fl oz) cream
fresh strawberries or cherries for decoration

Prepare the custard using custard powder, according to directions on the packet, using artificial sweetener. Cut the cake into strips and place in a glass serving bowl. Sprinkle with the sherry and top with the sliced peaches. Spoon the custard over the peaches and refrigerate until cool.

Cut the jelly into small cubes and spread over the custard. Whip the cream and pipe it over the trifle. Decorate with the strawberries or cherries.

BREAD AND BUTTER CUSTARD

This standard favourite could be tried with wholegrain bread.

Serves 6

One serve contains	
Carbohydrate	11 g
Calories	130
Kilojoules	550

2 eggs
2½ cups (20 fl oz) milk
¼ teaspoon vanilla essence
½ teaspoon liquid artificial sweetener
2 tablespoons sultanas
2 thin slices buttered bread
grated nutmeg

Preheat the oven to 150°C (300°F/Gas 2). Beat the eggs, milk, vanilla essence and sweetener together. Add the sultanas, pour into a greased ovenproof dish. Cut the buttered bread into finger-length pieces. Place them on top of the custard and sprinkle with the grated nutmeg.

Stand the dish in a tray of hot water and cook for 30 minutes or until the custard has set. Remove the dish immediately from the hot water to prevent further cooking.

ORANGES SEVILLE

Serves 8

One serve contains	
Carbohydrate	16 g
Calories	318
Kilojoules	1330

8 large oranges
4 cups (1 litre) vanilla ice cream
1 cup (8 fl oz) frozen concentrated orange juice, thawed
3 tablespoons Cointreau liqueur
mint sprigs for decoration

Cut off the tops of the oranges and scoop out the flesh (the flesh is not used in this recipe, purée and serve as a delicious drink).

Soften the ice cream and mix in the concentrated orange juice and liqueur. Spoon into the orange shells (do not overfill as the filling will expand slightly during freezing). Replace the orange tops and place oranges in freezer. Remove oranges about 1 hour before serving time to soften slightly. Decorate each with a little sprig of mint.

CAKES, BISCUITS AND BREADS

This is the all-time favourite cake recipe:

The Cake You Can Have (and Eat It Too!)

0 cups sugar
0 cups self-raising flour
0 teaspoons salt
a dash of nothing

Combine all ingredients, cook and serve as required. It is easy to make, economical and non-fattening. There is no washing of dishes and second helpings are never a problem.

To most of the recipes in this section we have added wholemeal flour and fruit, to boost their fibre content. The wholemeal flour gives a slightly nutty flavour and may be used to substitute for half of the white flour in any of your favourite cake recipes.

The cakes and biscuits have been sweetened with fruits instead of sugar. Small amounts of artificial sweetener have been added to bring the flavour as close to the original product as possible. Of course sweetness is a matter of choice, so add the liquid sweetener very gradually to the batter. It should taste a little sweeter than you would like the baked cakes and biscuits to taste as some sweetness is lost during cooking.

We have included in this section delicious bread recipes developed by the Bread Research Institute of Australia. Make the bread absolutely irresistible by serving it hot, straight from the oven. Do not hesitate to bake up generous batches — just serve enough for one meal and wrap and freeze the rest. Breads freeze beautifully and can be thawed and refrozen without damage. To freshen bread, brush the crust all over with milk and heat in the oven.

In all recipes, it is important to sift the flour before you measure. Spoon into a measuring cup and level off with a knife. This will make a big difference to the final result.

GRANDMA'S 'HAND-ME-DOWN' CHRISTMAS CAKE

This cake will add to the mistletoe magic!

Yields 50 slices

One slice contains	
Carbohydrate	24 g
Calories	135
Kilojoules	565

1½ cups (7½ oz) dates
1½ cups (8 oz) raisins
1½ cups (7 oz) currants
1½ cups (7 oz) dried pineapple
1½ cups (7 oz) dried figs
3 cups (24 fl oz) water
1½ cups (6 oz) wholemeal flour
3 cups (12 oz) sifted self-raising flour
¾ cup (6 fl oz) polyunsaturated oil
¾ cup (3 oz) cashew nuts, chopped

Chop fruit; soak in the water for 1 hour. Drain off water, reserve ½ cup.

Mix the flour, reserved water and oil to a soft dough. Add the fruit and mix thoroughly. Spread the mixture into a greased 25 cm (10 in) square cake tin. Cover with foil.

Bake for 3½ hours in 130°C (275°F/Gas 1) oven or when an inserted skewer comes out clean. Remove the foil 30 minutes before the end of cooking. Cut into 50 slices before serving.

SWISS APPLE CAKE (photograph on page 2)

Yields 8 slices

One serve contains	
Carbohydrate	18 g
Calories	114
Kilojoules	480

2 large cooking apples
2 tablespoons raisins or sultanas
⅓ cup (2½ fl oz) water
¾ teaspoon mixed spice
1 egg, separated
pinch of salt
½ teaspoon grated orange rind
1 cup (4 oz) sifted self-raising flour
½ cup (4 fl oz) milk
½ teaspoon vanilla essence
1 tablespoon oil
1 teaspoon liquid artificial sweetener

Preheat the oven to 180°C (350°F/Gas 4). Peel, core and slice the apples. Combine the sliced apples, raisins or sultanas, water and mixed spice in a saucepan. Cover and cook until the apples are tender. Drain off water.

Beat the egg white with the salt until stiff peaks form. Add the egg yolk and orange rind. Beat well. Fold in the sifted flour alternately with the remaining liquids.

Pour the mixture into a greased 15 cm (6 in) cake tin. Cover with the cooked apple, and bake for 30–35 minutes until set and golden.

BASIC BUTTERCAKE

Yields 12 slices

One slice contains	
Carbohydrate	16 g
Calories	167
Kilojoules	700

125 g (4 oz) butter or margarine
½ teaspoon vanilla essence
2 teaspoons liquid artificial sweetener
¼ cup (1 oz) wholemeal self-raising flour
2 eggs
1¾ cups (7 oz) sifted self-raising white flour
¾ cup (6 fl oz) milk

Preheat the oven to 180°C (350°F/Gas 4). Cream the butter. Add the vanilla, sweetener and wholemeal flour, beat well. Add the eggs one at a time, beating well after each addition. Fold in the flour alternately with the milk (begin and end with the flour).

Pour into a greased loaf tin or 18 cm (7 in) square cake tin. Bake for 30–35 minutes or until a skewer comes out clean. Cut into 12 slices.

Variations

Orange Cake: Omit vanilla. Add the grated rind and juice of 1 orange with sufficient milk to make up to the ¾ cup liquid. (17 g carbohydrate per slice).

Lemon Cake: Substitute vanilla for grated rind of 1 lemon. The best flavour is obtained when the rind is creamed with the butter. (16 g carbohydrate per slice).

Coconut Cake: Add ½ cup (1½ oz) coconut to the mixture. (16 g carbohydrate per slice).

Sultana or Raisin Cake: Sift ½ teaspoon mixed spice with the flour. Add 1 cup (6 oz) sultanas or chopped raisins. Cut into 18 slices. (1 g carbohydrate per slice).

Spice Cake: Sift 1 teaspoon nutmeg, ½ teaspoon cinnamon and ¼ teaspoon ground cloves with the flour. (16 g carbohydrate per slice).

Patty Cakes: Cook in 24 greased patty tins for 20 minutes. When quite cold, frost the cakes with Frosted Crème on page 109.

Chocolate Cake: Sift 2 tablespoons cocoa powder with the flour. Add more milk if batter is too dry. (16 g carbohydrate per slice).

Wholemeal Cake: Substitute ¾ cup white flour for wholemeal flour. A little more milk may be needed. (16 g carbohydrate per slice).

Crunchy Nut Cake: Sprinkle ⅓ cup (1½ oz) chopped nuts and ½ teaspoon cinnamon onto wholemeal cake variation before cooking. (17 g carbohydrate per slice).

SESAME CHEESE FANCIES

These will make cheesey dippers or simply tasty snacks on their own.

Yields 40 small biscuits

One biscuit contains	
Carbohydrate	2 g
Calories	30
Kilojoules	126

1 cup (4 oz) wholemeal flour
¼ teaspoon salt
pinch cayenne pepper
1 tablespoon butter
125 g (4 oz) tasty cheese, finely grated
1 egg
sesame seeds

Preheat the oven to 200°C (400°F/Gas 6). Place flour, salt and cayenne pepper in a bowl. Rub in the butter. Stir in the cheese and beaten egg to make a stiff dough. Add up to 1 tablespoon of cold water if the dough is too dry.

Knead the dough into a ball and roll out on a lightly floured board until 3 mm (⅛ in) thick. Cut into fancy shapes, prick each with a fork and place on a greased baking sheet. Brush the tops of the biscuits with water and sprinkle with sesame seeds. Bake for 6–8 minutes until golden.

HOLIDAY COOKIES (photograph on page 111)

These biscuits freeze and travel well.

Yields 24 biscuits

One biscuit contains	
Carbohydrate	8 g
Calories	106
Kilojoules	445

90 g (3 oz) butter
1 cup (4 oz) wholemeal flour
1 egg, lightly beaten
1 teaspoon grated orange rind
½ teaspoon vanilla essence
1 teaspoon baking powder
1 cup (5 oz) chopped salted peanuts
1 cup (1 oz) cornflakes, lightly crushed
1 cup (3 oz) rolled oats
1 teaspoon mixed spice
½ cup (4 fl oz) milk
1 tablespoon liquid artificial sweetener

Preheat the oven to 200°C (400°F/Gas 6). Using a wooden spoon beat the butter until creamy. Mix in 1 tablespoon of the flour. Add the beaten egg, vanilla and orange rind. Beat well.

Mix in the remaining ingredients. Place in spoonfuls on a greased baking sheet and bake for 20–25 minutes.

THE BAKEHOUSE SPECIAL

A traditional date loaf which never fails.

Yields 18 slices

One slice contains	
Carbohydrate	16 g
Calories	97
Kilojoules	405

1 cup (8 fl oz) boiling water
1 cup (5 oz) chopped dates
60 g (2 oz) butter or margarine
1 teaspoon bicarbonate of soda (baking soda)
pinch mixed spice
2–3 drops liquid artificial sweetener
1 egg, beaten
2 cups sifted self-raising flour

Preheat oven to 180°C (350°F/Gas 4). Combine the boiling water, dates, butter, soda, mixed spice and sweetener in a large bowl. Cool slightly.

Mix in the beaten egg and flour. Pour into a greased loaf tin and bake for 25–30 minutes, or until an inserted skewer comes out clean.

RAVE-ON RAISIN CAKE

A cake high in fibre and natural goodness.

Yields 20 slices

One slice contains	
Carbohydrate	18 g
Calories	178
Kilojoules	745

250 g (8 oz) butter or margarine
1 cup (5 oz) raisins, chopped
rind of 1 orange
½ cup (4 fl oz) orange juice
1 tablespoon liquid artificial sweetener
3 eggs, lightly beaten
1½ cups (6 oz) sifted self-raising flour
1 cup (4 oz) self-raising wholemeal flour
½ cup (½ oz) unprocessed bran
½ cup (4 fl oz) milk

Preheat the oven to 190°C (375°F/Gas 5). Combine the butter, raisins, orange rind and juice in a saucepan. Slowly bring to the boil and allow to simmer for 2 minutes. Leave to cool.

Add the sweetener and beaten eggs. Mix well. Mix the dry ingredients together. Stir into the raisin mixture with the milk. Pour into a greased 20 cm (8 in) cake tin. Bake for 40–45 minutes or when an inserted skewer comes out clean.

BANANA WACKY CAKE

A favourite of ours that we like topped with Frosted Crème.

Yields 18 slices

One slice contains	
Carbohydrate	17 g
Calories	102
Kilojoules	425

1 cup (4 oz) wholemeal flour
1 cup (4 oz) sifted flour
2 teaspoons baking powder
¼ teaspoon bicarbonate of soda (baking soda)
¼ teaspoon mixed spice
60 g (2 oz) butter
1 egg
½ cup (2½ oz) chopped dates
3 bananas, mashed
⅓ cup (2½ oz) milk
2½ teaspoons liquid artificial sweetener

Frosted Crème

125 g (4 oz) cream cheese
1 tablespoon cream
1 teaspoon vanilla essence
¼ teaspoon salt
liquid artificial sweetener to taste
toasted coconut

Preheat the oven to 180°C (350°F/Gas 4). Mix together the dry ingredients. Using a wooden spoon, cream the butter with 1 tablespoon of the flour mixture. Add the egg and beat well. Stir in the dates and mashed bananas. Lastly fold in the remaining flour mixture alternately with the milk and sweetener.

Spread the mixture evenly into a greased 23 cm (9 in) ring tin and bake for 45–50 minutes. Allow the cake to cool before spreading with Frosted Crème. Sprinkle with toasted coconut.

Frosted Crème: Blend all of the ingredients for the Crème together. Sweeten as desired. (Frosted Crème adds 28 calories/117 kilojoules per slice.)

BUTTERNUT PUMPKIN CAKE (photograph opposite)

If you enjoy the sweet nutty flavour of pumpkin, this cake will be irresistible.

Yields 18 slices

One slice contains	
Carbohydrate	18 g
Calories	147
Kilojoules	615

125 g (4 oz) butter
½ cup (4 fl oz) freshly squeezed orange juice
1 cup (8 oz) mashed cooked butternut pumpkin (not too dry)
1 cup (5 oz) chopped dates
1 egg, lightly beaten
½ cup (2 oz) chopped walnuts
½ teaspoon mixed spice
2 cups (8 oz) sifted self-raising flour
flaked almonds

Preheat the oven to 180°C (350°F/Gas 4). Melt the butter, allow to cool slightly. Add the orange juice, pumpkin, dates, beaten egg, walnuts, and mixed spice.

Fold in the sifted flour. (If the dough is too dry add up to ¼ cup of milk.) Pour into a greased 23 x 10 cm loaf tin. Bake for 45–50 minutes. Scatter flaked almonds on top.

BUTTERMILK PRUNE CAKE (photograph opposite)

Yields 20 slices

One slice contains	
Carbohydrate	15 g
Calories	138
Kilojoules	580

1 cup (4 oz) sifted white flour
1 teaspoon bicarbonate of soda (baking soda)
¼ teaspoon salt
1 teaspoon mixed spice
½ teaspoon allspice
¼ teaspoon ground cloves
½ cup (2 oz) wholemeal flour
125 g (4 oz) butter or margarine
1 tablespoon liquid artificial sweetener
2 eggs
1 cup (6 oz) chopped dried prunes
⅓ cup (4 oz) chopped almonds
⅔ cup (5 fl oz) buttermilk

Preheat the oven to 180°C (350°F/Gas 4). Sift the white flour with the soda, salt and spices. Stir in the wholemeal flour. Cream the butter. Mix in the sweetener and 3 tablespoons of the flour mixture and beat well. Add eggs, one at a time, mixing well after each addition. Stir in chopped prunes and almonds. Fold in dry ingredients alternately with the buttermilk (the mixture will be quite dry).

Pour into a greased 25 cm (10 in) round cake tin. Bake for 30–35 minutes or until an inserted skewer comes out clean. If desired, ice with Frosted Crème (see page 109).

PIKELETS

Yields 24 pikelets

One pikelet contains	
Carbohydrate	4 g
Calories	35
Kilojoules	145

1 cup (4 oz) sifted self-raising flour
1 egg
¾ cup (6 fl oz) milk
30 g (1 oz) butter, melted
1 teaspoon liquid artificial sweetener

Sift flour into a mixing bowl and make a well in the centre. Combine remaining ingredients; gradually add to flour stirring continually with a wooden spoon. Beat until smooth.

Preheat frying pan. Add just enough butter to lightly grease the base. Drop batter by dessertspoonfuls on to heated surface. Turn the pikelets when bubbles begin to appear on the surface. Remove when golden brown and cool on a clean tea-towel placed over a wire cooling rack.

Buttermilk Prune Cake (page 110); Holiday Cookies (page 108); Oaties (page 113); Butternut Pumpkin Cake (page 110)

Hobbit Log (page 110); Skating Mice (page 118); Marshmallows (page 119); Rosy's Punch (page 121); Butterflies (page 118)

OATIES (photograph on page 111)

Little Scottish treasures, full of natural goodness, oaties are easy to make and freeze well.

Yields 25 squares

One square contains	
Carbohydrate	17 g
Calories	125
Kilojoules	525

1½ cups (6 oz) wholemeal flour
1½ cups (4½ oz) rolled oats
¾ cup (2½ oz) coconut
⅓ cup (2 oz) chopped raisins
⅓ cup (2 oz) chopped sultanas
¾ cup (4 oz) chopped dates
½ teaspoon salt
2 tablespoons lemon juice
½ cup (4 fl oz) polyunsaturated oil
1 cup (8 fl oz) skim milk
1 teaspoon vanilla essence

Preheat the oven to 180°C (350°F/Gas 4). Combine the flour, oats, coconut, raisins, sultanas, dates and salt in a bowl.

Mix the lemon juice, oil, milk and vanilla together and add to the dry ingredients. Mix well. Press into a greased Swiss roll tin and bake for 45–50 minutes. Cut into 25 squares while still hot.

APPLE SLICE

Sultanas sweeten the pie apple during cooking and so only a small amount of artificial sweetener is needed.

Yields 24 squares

One square contains	
Carbohydrate	16 g
Calories	115
Kilojoules	480

Pastry

2 cups (8 oz) wholemeal self-raising flour
1 cup (4 oz) white flour
2 tablespoons custard powder
pinch salt
125 g (4 oz) butter or margarine
1 egg, lightly beaten
½ cup (4 fl oz) milk
½ teaspoon liquid artificial sweetener

Apple Filling

3 cups (1 lb 5 oz) solid pack pie apple
½ teaspoon finely grated lemon rind
3 tablespoons sultanas or chopped raisins
½ teaspoon liquid artificial sweetener

Pastry: Preheat the oven to 200°C (400°F/Gas 6). Sift flours, custard powder and salt into a bowl. Add the grist left in the sifter. Rub in the butter until mixture resembles fine breadcrumbs. Combine egg, milk and sweetener, add to flour and mix to a firm dough.

Turn out on to a floured surface, knead lightly. Cut the pastry in half, roll out half the pastry to line the base of a greased 28 x 18 cm (11 x 7 in) lamington tin. Spread prepared filling evenly over the pastry. Roll out the remaining pastry to cover apple. Place over the apple and trim the edges (leave a small amount of pastry overhanging to allow for shrinkage). Brush top with a little extra milk and bake for 15 minutes or until top is golden brown; reduce heat to moderate and cook further 20–25 minutes.

Allow to cool in the tin. When cold remove from tin and cut into 24 squares.

Apple Filling: Combine ingredients and mix well. Adjust sweetness if desired.

FRUIT SCONES

The wholemeal flour adds a delicious nutty change to the basic scone. Vary the fruit with chopped dates, raisins or currants.

Yields 14 scones

One serve contains	
Carbohydrate	18 g
Calories	104
Kilojoules	435

1 cup (4 oz) wholemeal self-raising flour
1 cup (4 oz) white self-raising flour
½ teaspoon mixed spice
30 g (1 oz) butter or margarine
½ cup (3 oz) sultanas
¾ cup (6 fl oz) milk
1 teaspoon liquid artificial sweetener
extra 2 tablespoons flour for kneading

Preheat the oven to 230–250°C (450–500°F). Sift the flours and spice into a large bowl, include the grist from the wholemeal flour. Lightly rub in the butter until the mixture resembles fine breadcrumbs. Add the sultanas. Using a round-bladed knife, quickly mix in the milk to make a soft dough.

Turn on to a floured surface and knead lightly until smooth. Press dough out to 2.5 cm (1 in) thick and cut into rounds using a floured scone cutter. Place on a greased baking sheet, glaze with a little milk or water and bake for 12–15 minutes.

The scones are cooked if they sound hollow when tapped. Cool on a wire rack.

POTATO PASTRY

Leftover pastry can be wrapped and refrigerated for up to 3 days.

Makes a two-crust 23 cm (9 in) pie shell

Total recipe contains	
Carbohydrate	183 g
Calories	1157
Kilojoules	4850

1½ cups (12 oz) cold mashed cooked potato
1 egg
2 tablespoons water
1½ cups (6 oz) wholemeal flour
½ cup (1½ oz) skim milk powder
½ teaspoon salt
¼ teaspoon ground sage
pinch onion powder
freshly ground pepper

Combine potato, egg and water in a bowl. Beat well. Mix in remaining ingredients. Allow to stand for 30 minutes.

Use for any savoury pies.

WHOLEMEAL PASTRY

Makes enough for one 21 cm (8 in) pie dish

Total recipe contains	
Carbohydrate	135 g
Calories	1402
Kilojoules	5870

1 cup (4 oz) wholemeal flour
½ cup (2 oz) self-raising flour
100 g (3½ oz) butter or margarine
1 egg yolk
3 tablespoons cold water

Mix the flours together in a bowl. Using the fingertips, lightly rub in the butter until the mixture resembles fine breadcrumbs.

Mix together the egg yolk and water. Add to the flour mixture to make a stiff dough. Knead lightly and form into a ball. Wrap in foil and store in the refrigerator until required.

ENGLISH MUFFINS (photograph on page 57)

Yields 12 muffins

One muffin contains	
Carbohydrate	33 g
Calories	173
Kilojoules	725

1 cup (8 fl oz) milk
2 cups (8 oz) wholemeal flour
2 cups (8 oz) white flour
2 teaspoons sugar
1½ teaspoons salt
1½ tablespoons salad oil
20 g (1 tablespoon) compressed yeast
⅓ cup (2½ fl oz) lukewarm water
¼ cup (1 oz) maize or cornmeal

Scald milk, then cool to lukewarm. Combine flours, sugar and salt in a bowl. Mix salad oil and milk together. Disperse yeast in water.

Make a well in the centre of the dry ingredients, add milk and water mixtures. Mix to a soft dough (with a scone-like consistency). Turn dough on to a lightly floured board, knead until smooth and springy (about 10 minutes). Form into a ball. Place dough in a greased bowl, turn over to grease the top, cover with tea towel and let rise in a warm place until doubled in bulk. Punch down dough, turn out on a board dusted with cornmeal. Roll out dough to 1 cm (½ in) thick circle and cut into rounds with a 7 cm (3 in) biscuit cutter. Place muffins, cornmeal side up about 5 cm (2 in) apart on ungreased oven trays, lightly dusted with cornmeal.

Cover lightly and let rise in warm place until puffy — approximately 45 minutes. Bake muffins on a lightly greased griddle or in a lightly greased electric frypan preheated to 130°C (275°F/Gas 1). Cool on wire racks.

Courtesy of Bread Research Institute of Australia.

WHOLESOME BRAN MUFFINS

Yields 30 muffins

One muffin contains	
Carbohydrate	7 g
Calories	40
Kilojoules	165

1 cup (4 oz) wholemeal flour
2 cups (2½ oz) unprocessed bran
3½ teaspoons baking powder
1 cup (5 oz) chopped dates
1½ cups (12 fl oz) milk
3 teaspoons liquid artificial sweetener

Preheat the oven to 220°C (425°F/Gas 7). Lightly mix all of the ingredients together in a bowl.

Place the mixture into greased patty cake tins. Bake for 15 minutes or until a light golden brown.

BACON BREAD

Yields 2 loaves

One slice contains	
Carbohydrate	18 g
Calories	102
Kilojoules	425

6 cups (1½ lb) flour
1 teaspoon salt
60 g (2 oz) bacon, chopped
60 g (2 oz) romano cheese, grated
45 g (1½ oz) compressed yeast
1¾ cups (14 fl oz) lukewarm water (variable)

Mix flour, salt, bacon and cheese together in a large bowl. Disperse yeast in 1 cup of the water and add to the dry ingredients with the remaining water to make a soft dough. Knead on a lightly floured board for 5–10 minutes until dough is satiny and smooth.

Divide dough into 4 pieces, mould and place into two well-greased loaf tins. Cover with a clean cloth and a piece of plastic, put in a warm place until dough has almost doubled (about 30 minutes).

Preheat the oven to 230°C (450°F/Gas 8). Bake for 30 minutes. Cut into 30 even slices.

Courtesy of Bread Research Institute of Australia.

WHOLEMEAL BREAD

Yields 2 loaves

One slice contains	
Carbohydrate	17 g
Calories	79
Kilojoules	330

45 g (1½ oz) compressed yeast
⅔ cup (6 fl oz) water
6 cups (1½ lb) wholemeal flour
2 teaspoons salt
1 teaspoon sugar
2 teaspoons lard or salad oil
1⅔ cups water (variable)

Preheat the oven to 230°C (450°F/Gas 8). Dissolve the yeast in ⅔ cup of the water.

Sift the flour into a large bowl, add the salt and sugar. Rub in lard or salad oil. Make a well in the centre and add the yeast mixture and sufficient water to make a soft dough (with a scone dough consistency). Turn this on to a lightly floured board. Knead thoroughly for 10 minutes. Cover with a clean cloth and rest for 5 minutes.

Divide dough in 2 and shape each piece into a loaf. Place in 2 well-greased loaf pans and stand in a warm place until dough rises above the top of the pan (approximately 30 minutes). Bake at 230°C (450°F/Gas 8) for 20 minutes. Cut each loaf into 16 slices.

Note: To make brown bread, use 3 cups of white flour and 3 cups of wholemeal flour. This mixture will produce a larger loaf.

Courtesy of Bread Research Institute of Australia.

HERBED BREAD

One slice contains	
Carbohydrate	8 g
Calories	65
Kilojoules	270

90 g (3 oz) butter or margarine
3 cloves garlic, crushed
1–2 teaspoons dried mixed herbs (or 2 tablespoons fresh if available)
¼ teaspoon salt
1 long loaf French bread (preferably mixed grain)

Beat the butter until soft (but not melted). Mix in the garlic, herbs and salt. Using a sharp bread knife, cut the bread into 2 cm (¾ in) slices, keeping the loaf in its original shape. Spread each slice with the herbed butter and re-position.

Wrap the loaf in foil and refrigerate until needed. Heat in a preheated 190°C (375°F/Gas 5) oven for 15–20 minutes, or until piping hot.

CHEESEY GARLIC BREAD

One slice contains	
Carbohydrate	8 g
Calories	87
Kilojoules	365

2 French bread sticks
125 g (4 oz) butter
1 cup (4 oz) grated matured cheese
4 spring onions (scallions), finely chopped
4 cloves garlic, crushed
1 tablespoon chopped parsley

Cream the butter, cheese, onions, garlic and parsley together. Cut the bread sticks into 1 cm (½ in) slices, retaining the shape of the loaf.

Place on a sheet of aluminium foil. Spread the butter generously on both sides of the slices, press the loaf back into shape and wrap loosely in foil.

Bake in a hot oven 220°C (425°F/Gas 7) 20–25 minutes or until the bread is crisp on the outside. Serve hot.

Courtesy of Bread Research Institute of Australia.

SWEET ALTERNATIVES

Today, adults, teenagers and children consume more food away from the family table. More often than not these snacks are composed of sugar and fat with very few essential nutrients. If you are forced to eat snack foods it is important to try and make your snack as nutritious as possible. A few examples follow:

natural yoghurt
fresh fruit or fruit salad
fruit juice
dried fruit
nuts
cottage cheese
wholemeal scones
carton of milk
small bread roll

As every child deserves a party this section has been devoted to them. Some traditional party foods (of course without sugar) are here as well as two recipes for jam. We do not really recommend for diabetics the many 'diabetic' jams on the market (see page 14 for suitable commercial products). Substitute 1 teaspoon of our Strawberry and Apple Spread or Apricot Jam, as the carbohydrate content is considered negligible.

STRAWBERRY AND APPLE SPREAD

500 g (1 lb) fresh strawberries
1½ cups (12 fl oz) unsweetened pie apple
2 tablespoons lemon juice
2 tablespoons orange juice
⅔ cup (5 fl oz) hot water
1½ tablespoons diabetic strawberry jelly crystals
liquid artificial sweetener (optional)

Total recipe contains	
Carbohydrate	83 g
Calories	333
Kilojoules	1395

Place the strawberries, pie apple and lemon juice in a large saucepan. Simmer for 30 minutes, stirring frequently. Add the hot water to the jelly crystals. Stir until dissolved. Remove the fruit mixture from the heat and stir in the jelly. Sweeten to taste.

Bottle and seal while still hot. Store in the refrigerator for up to 3 weeks.

APRICOT JAM

A nutritious alternative to jam to serve with bread, scones, crêpes and cakes.

125 g (4 oz) dried apricots
1 cup (8 fl oz) orange juice
125 g (4 oz) dried apples
3 cups (24 fl oz) water
1 tablespoon lemon juice
3 teaspoons diabetic lemon jelly crystals
⅓ cup (2½ fl oz) boiling water
liquid artificial sweetener (optional)

Total recipe contains	
Carbohydrate	198 g
Calories	766
Kilojoules	3210

Soak the apricots in orange juice and the apples in water overnight. Next day, combine the apricots, apples, remaining liquid and lemon juice in a large saucepan. Simmer uncovered for 1½ hours. Mash the fruit to a pulp.

Add the boiling water to the jelly crystals. Mix until dissolved. Stir the jelly mixture into the jam. Sweeten to taste.

Bottle and seal the jam while still hot. Store in the refrigerator for up to 3 weeks.

SKATING MICE (photograph on page 112)

The 'mice' can be prepared well ahead for the after-school birthday party. Choose a jelly flavour to match your party colour scheme.

Serves 6

One serve contains	
Carbohydrate	14 g
Calories	166
Kilojoules	695

1 x 500 ml (16 fl oz) diabetic jelly prepared and allowed to set
3 fresh ripe pears, peeled and cut in half (or canned unsweetened pears)
6 blanched almonds, halved or flaked
12 currants
1½ glacé cherries, washed
1 long piece angelica, washed
¾ cup (6 fl oz) cream

Using a knife, chop up the jelly until quite fine. Spoon into individual glass dishes or one large shallow dish.

Place the pear halves on top of each bed of jelly and decorate as 'mice', using the almonds for the ears and the currants for eyes. Shape the cherry quarters into noses and position on mice. Cut the angelica into 6 strips and use as tails.

Whip the cream and pipe rosettes around the edge of the dish or dishes. Refrigerate until serving time.

BUTTERFLIES (photograph on page 112)

Yields 24

One 'butterfly' contains	
Carbohydrate	8 g
Calories	120
Kilojoules	500

125 g (4 oz) butter or margarine
2 teaspoons liquid artificial sweetener
½ teaspoon vanilla essence
2 cups (8 oz) sifted self-raising flour
2 eggs
¾ cup (6 fl oz) milk
1 cup (8 fl oz) cream, whipped
1 prepared diabetic jelly (raspberry or strawberry)

Preheat the oven to 190°C (375°F/Gas 5). Cream the butter until soft. Mix in the sweetener, vanilla and two tablespoons of the sifted flour. Add the eggs, one at a time, beating well after each addition. Fold in the remaining flour alternately with the milk.

Spoon mixture into 24 greased patty tins. Bake for 15–20 minutes. Allow to cool on a wire rack.

When the cakes are completely cold, use a sharp knife to cut the tops off the cakes. Cut each top in half lengthwise to make the 'butterfly wings'. Set aside. Fill each cake with a heaped teaspoon of whipped cream. Replace the 'wings' and top with a little jelly between the wings.

CHOCOLATE CRACKLES

Yields 15 crackles

One crackle contains	
Carbohydrate	4 g
Calories	89
Kilojoules	375

125 g (4 oz) copha
½ cup (1½ oz) desiccated coconut
2 cups (2 oz) rice bubbles
1½ tablespoons cocoa powder
3 teaspoons liquid artificial sweetener

Melt the copha and stir in the other ingredients. Divide evenly into 15 paper cases. Store in the refrigerator.

HOBBIT LOG (photograph on page 112)

A natural sweet from the land of hobbits.

Yields 25 slices

One slice contains	
Carbohydrate	20 g
Calories	128
Kilojoules	540

¾ cup (4 oz) dried apricots, chopped
½ cup (2½ oz) sultanas
½ cup (2½ oz) raisins, chopped
¼ cup (1½ oz) prunes, chopped
½ cup (2½ oz) dates, chopped
½ cup (4 fl oz) boiling water
⅓ cup (2 oz) chopped peanuts
2 teaspoons lemon juice
½ cup (1½ oz) coconut
⅓ cup (2½ oz) sunflower seeds
½ cup (1½ oz) skim milk powder
extra ¾ cup (2½ oz) coconut

Place the dried fruits into a bowl. Pour over boiling water. Allow to stand for 10 minutes to soften the fruit.

Add the peanuts, lemon juice, coconut, sunflower seeds and milk powder. Mix well. Form the mixture into a 5 cm (2 in) diameter log. Roll in the extra coconut. Wrap in foil and refrigerate. Cut into 25 even slices before serving.

MARSHMALLOWS (photograph on page 112)

These marshmallows are relatively low in calories or kilojoules. Ideal for when you are hungry between meals. Great for children's parties too!

Yields 20

One marshmallow contains	
Carbohydrate	1 g
Calories	15
Kilojoules	65

3 tablespoons gelatine
1½ cups (12 fl oz) boiling water
1 packet diabetic strawberry jelly crystals
1 cup (8 fl oz) hot water
liquid artificial sweetener, optional
¾ cup (2 oz) toasted coconut

Combine the gelatine and boiling water in a saucepan, stir until dissolved. Bring to the boil and simmer gently for 6–8 minutes.

In a large mixing bowl, prepare the jelly according to packet instructions using only 1 cup hot water (making double strength jelly). Add the dissolved gelatine and refrigerate until just beginning to set.

Whip the jelly until doubled in volume (add sweetener if desired) then pour into a wetted lamington tin. Chill until set. Cut into 20 squares and roll in toasted coconut. Store in refrigerator.

FROZEN BANANA SPEARS

Yields 6

One 'spear' contains	
Carbohydrate	15 g
Calories	119
Kilojoules	500

3 firm bananas
½ cup (4 oz) non-fat natural yoghurt
⅓ cup (1 oz) coconut
⅓ cup (1½ oz) chopped nuts

Peel and cut the bananas in half cross-wise. Spear each cut end with an ice cream stick and freeze (overnight if possible). When frozen, roll each banana spear in the yoghurt followed by coconut and nuts. Return to the freezer and freeze until solid.

THIRST QUENCHERS

This section deals with some interesting sugar-free drinks, for special celebrations or just to quench the thirst on a summer's day.

For a festive occasion, serve ice-cold lemonade or a fruit punch. To keep a punch cold without diluting, add frozen juice cubes or line a large punch bowl with crushed ice and place the smaller bowl inside.

The Buttermilk Blender is just one of the many combinations using buttermilk and fruit. It is a great way to drink buttermilk whether you are a fan or a first-timer. Combine buttermilk with any fruit juice or artificially sweetened soft drink or try equal parts of buttermilk and tomato juice, seasoning with Worcestershire sauce, salt and pepper.

For a taste-tingling refreshment, blend yoghurt with fresh fruit, fruit juice or vegetable juice and serve chilled over ice.

BUTTERMILK BLENDER

Yields 4 glasses

2 cups (16 fl oz) buttermilk
2 medium oranges, peeled and chopped (remove seeds)
2 bananas, roughly chopped

One glass contains	
Carbohydrate	26 g
Calories	142
Kilojoules	595

Combine ingredients in a blender. Blend until light and frothy and pour into glasses.

Variation

Omit bananas. Stir the pulp of 2 passionfruit into the mixture after blending, pour into glasses. (Carbohydrate 12 g/Calories 98/Kilojoules 410.)

APRICOT FIZZ

Serves 2

¾ cup (6 fl oz) apricot juice
¾ cup (6 fl oz) artificially sweetened Bitter Lemon
squeeze lemon juice
crushed ice
kiwi fruit for decoration

One serve contains	
Carbohydrate	9 g
Calories	41
Kilojoules	170

Combine apricot juice, Bitter Lemon and lemon juice. Place crushed ice in 2 tall glasses. Pour over apricot drink. Decorate each glass with a slice of kiwi fruit and serve immediately.

VEGETABLE REFRESHER

Yields 4 glasses

2 cups (16 fl oz) tomato juice
1 medium carrot, roughly chopped
1 stick celery, roughly chopped
2 sprigs parsley (optional)
1 tablespoon lemon juice
1 teaspoon Worcestershire sauce
½ teaspoon salt

One serve contains	
Carbohydrate	6 g
Calories	36
Kilojoules	150

Combine all ingredients in a blender or processor; blend on high speed until smooth. Pour into 4 glasses and serve immediately.

GINGER QUENCHER

Yields 4 glasses

One glass contains	
Carbohydrate	17 g
Calories	82
Kilojoules	345

1 cup (8 fl oz) artificially sweetened Dry Ginger Ale
1 cup (8 oz) non-fat natural yoghurt
2 large or 3 small ripe pears, peeled, cored and chopped

Combine all ingredients in a blender. Blend until smooth and thick.

Variation

Substitute 2 medium apples for the pears.

ROSY'S PUNCH (photograph on page 112)

A taste-tingling refreshment that is low in both carbohydrate and energy count.

Yields 10 glasses

One glass contains	
Carbohydrate	3 g
Calories	14
Kilojoules	60

pulp of 4 passionfruit
1 tablespoon chopped mint
juice of 2–3 lemons
few drops Angostura Bitters
6 cups (1.5 litres) artificially sweetened lemonade
1 lemon, thinly sliced

Combine the passionfruit, mint, lemon juice and Angostura Bitters in a large jug or bowl.

Just before serving add ice and lemonade. Decorate with fresh lemon slices and serve immediately.

Variation

Substitute half the quantity of lemonade for artificially sweetened dry ginger ale.

LEMONADE

Serves 6

One serve contains	
Carbohydrate	6 g
Calories	25
Kilojoules	105

6 medium lemons
2½ cups (20 fl oz) water
liquid artificial sweetener to taste
ice and mint sprigs for decoration

Cut the lemons into small pieces (leave the skin on). Combine the lemons and the water in a blender or processor (best to do in 2–3 lots). Blend thoroughly, then strain. Sweeten to taste.

Serve in a jug with the ice and mint sprigs.

HAWAIIAN COFFEE

Serves 4

One serve contains	
Carbohydrate	20 g
Calories	116
Kilojoules	485

1 cup (8 fl oz) water, chilled
1½ tablespoons instant coffee
1¾ cups (14 fl oz) pineapple juice, chilled
4 scoops vanilla ice cream

Combine the water, coffee and pineapple juice in a bowl or jug. Stir until the coffee dissolves.

Add the ice cream and beat well (use a rotary beater). Pour into 4 glasses and serve immediately.

Sprouting for Health

'Wanted! A vegetable that will grow in any climate, will rival meat in nutritive value, will mature in 3–5 days, may be planted any day of the year, will require neither soil nor sunshine, will rival tomatoes in Vitamin C, will be free of waste in preparation and can be cooked with as little fuel and as quickly as a . . . chop.'*

Sprouts can be grown just about anywhere. All you need is a clean container, a little water, seed and minimal effort to produce natural protein-packed sprouts, bursting with vitamins. Sprouts are tiny young shoots that emerge from seeds, legumes or grains on the way to becoming mature plants. A teaspoon of seed produces from one to two cups of sprouts, ready to be used in your salads and cooking.

They are an excellent fresh source of vitamins A, B complex, C, D, G and K and minerals such as calcium, magnesium, phosphorus and potassium. At the same time, sprouts are low in carbohydrate and are included among the free vegetables of a diabetic diet.

Not only do sprouts add nutritional value to your meals, they also add a wonderful variety of flavour and texture. Use in the way you would use lettuce – in salads, sandwiches and on crackers. They are also delicious in soups, drinks and stir-fried dishes. Mung bean sprouts form the basis for much Oriental cooking. Alfalfa (lucerne), clover, fenugreek, mung and lentil are some of the most commonly used and easiest to sprout. Each has its own distinctive flavour.

SPROUTING YOUR SEEDS

Everyone who has had any experience with sprouting usually has a favourite method. For us, it is simply using a wide-mouth 1 litre (4 cup) jar. Sprouting is a matter of maintaining the right temperature, amount of moisture and light conditions to enable the seed to swell, then burst its shell and start to grow. For good results, put your container in a dark spot such as in a cupboard, as the seeds need relative darkness to sprout.

How to Sprout

1. Choose a large wide-mouth jar.
2. Select good quality seeds, discarding any that are cracked, broken or discoloured. Use ½ cup of medium-sized seeds (mung beans) or 1 tablespoon of small seeds (alfalfa).
3. Rinse the seeds in a strainer. Place in the jar and cover with lukewarm water, soak overnight.
4. In the morning, pour off the water. The water now contains soluble vitamins and minerals so save it to use in your soups and gravies.
5. Cover the jar opening with cheese cloth or clean nylon stocking and secure with a rubber band.
6. Rinse and drain seeds morning and night, for 2–5 days. Each time shake the jar to distribute the seeds across the bottom and lay the jar on its side in a dark place.
7. To develop a healthy green colour in the sprouts, place in the sunlight for 3–12 hours.
8. The sprouts are now ready to eat! Replace the cheese cloth with the lid of the jar. Store in the refrigerator to prevent spoilage. They should be eaten within 5 days for maximum nutritive value and flavour.

* **Dr. Clive M. McKay**
Professor of Nutrition, Cornell University, United States.

HERBS 'n' SPICE and all things nice

Herbs and spices enhance and develop the natural flavour of food.

The delicate flavour of fresh herbs is unequalled and well worth the little effort needed to grow your own. The window sill in your kitchen is the ideal spot for a flourishing herb garden.

Spices are a little expensive as they are generally imported and best bought in small quantities. Both dried herbs and spices should be stored in a dark dry place to retain their freshness.

We have included a chart of the most commonly used herbs and spices. All spice racks have their limit! Some possible alternatives are listed for those herbs and spices not on your shelves.

	DESCRIPTION	USE	ALTERNATIVE
Allspice (ground pimento)	A spice resembling the combined flavours of nutmeg, cloves and cinnamon.	Pickling, preserving, boiled meats, puddings and cakes.	Combine ground nutmeg, cloves and cinnamon.
Balm	The strong lemon-scented leaves give it the popular name of 'lemon balm'.	Salads, fish, milk puddings, jellies and cool drinks. Add to a cup of tea.	Lemon juice and mint leaves.
Basil	The bright green leaves have a spicy clove-like aroma and taste.	Tomato dishes, zucchini, eggplant, pasta, pea soup and green salads.	
Bay Leaves	An ingredient of bouquet garni, bay leaves are glossy dark green leaves of laurel.	Soups, casseroles, patés and marinades.	Commercial bouquet garni.
Bouquet Garni	A combination of bayleaf, thyme, rosemary and parsley sprigs tied together.	Casseroles, stocks and soups.	A piece of bayleaf and a pinch of each of the herbs.
Caraway Seeds	These small seeds are brown and crescent-shaped and are marked with distinctive ridges.	Breads, cakes, vegetable dishes, cheese and dips.	
Cardamom	An Indian spice available in pods or powder. Crush pods to release flavour.	Curries, rice dishes, marinades, punches, cakes and Indian sweets.	
Cayenne Pepper	A mixture of red pepper or small hot chillies that have been dried and ground. Use sparingly.	Egg and cheese dishes, salmon, tuna.	A mild chilli powder.
Chervil	The fern-like leaves have a mild flavour of aniseed. It is similar to parsley, but more delicate.	Garnish, eggs, cheese, vegetables, poultry and fish.	Parsley.
Chilli Powder	Mainly ground chillis. Use with care to sharpen the flavour of food.	Chilli con Carne, Boston Baked Beans, sauces, Spanish rice, eggs and vegetables.	Cayenne pepper.

	DESCRIPTION	USE	ALTERNATIVE
Chives	The bright green stems have a mild onion flavour.	Salads, cooked vegetables, cheese, eggs, dips, rice and fish.	Shallots or spring onions (scallions).
Cinnamon	A sweet spice available in quills of the bark or in the ground form.	Steamed vegetables, cakes, puddings, coffee and stewed fruit.	Cassia.
Cloves	Hard dried flower buds, available whole or ground. Cloves have a penetrating spicy flavour.	Preserves, stewed apples, soups, stuffings, fruit cakes, decoration for leg of ham and clove-studded onions and oranges.	
Coriander	The ground seed has a warm spicy flavour. It is an ingredient in curry powder.	Fish, poultry and meat dishes, in cakes, pastry, bread and sprinkled over fruit.	Lemon peel and sage.
Cumin	With its pungent aroma, ground cumin gives a subtle Eastern character to food.	Meat casseroles, lentil soup, rice, cabbage and bean dishes, oriental cooking, fruit puddings and cakes.	
Dill	Similar to fennel in appearance and flavour but slightly milder. The leaves complement most foods.	Cabbage, cucumber, root vegetables, pastries, meat, fish and sauces.	Fennel.
Fennel	The aniseed flavour of the tops, bulb and seed make it extremely versatile.	Fish, eggs, stir-fried dishes, soups and salads.	Anise or dill.
Garam Masala	A mixture of ground spices used in Indian cooking. There are many versions, some with fragrant spices only, others with the addition of hot spices such as pepper.	Curries, fish, poultry, meat, vegetables.	Ground pepper, cloves and cinnamon.
Ginger	Green root ginger is used in savoury dishes, while ground ginger is in sweet and savoury dishes. Preserved and crystallised ginger contains large amounts of sugar.	Green ginger is used in Chinese cooking; ground ginger flavours biscuits, cakes, cooked fruit and desserts.	
Mace	The lacy covering on inner shell holding nutmeg, the flavour is similar to nutmeg but more delicate.	Marinades, brines, sauces, fish, lamb or veal.	Small amount of nutmeg.

	DESCRIPTION	USE	ALTERNATIVE
Marjoram	A strongly perfumed herb that teams well with thyme and sage.	Stuffing, poultry, meat loaves and casseroles, fish, vegetables, salad greens, dressing and tomato juice.	Small amount of oregano.
Mint	Adds a tangy freshness to sweet and savoury foods. It does not go well with other herbs.	Mint sauce or jelly for lamb, in steamed vegetables, salads, tomato, orange, pineapple, fruit salad, iced mint tea.	
Mixed Spice	A blend of ground spices including nutmeg, coriander, caraway, allspice, ginger and cinnamon.	Puddings, cakes, biscuits and cooked fruit.	A combination of the spices.
Mustard	Available powdered or prepared. Prepared mustard is the ground seed blended with other spices and vinegar.	Ground mustard is used in dressings, spreads, dips, devilled eggs and vegetables; prepared mustard is traditionally served with ham and beef and can also be added to cheese dishes, sauces and dressings.	
Nutmeg	Freshly grated or ready ground nutmeg is an aromatic spice stimulating to the palate.	Tops egg flips, milk puddings, and spikes patè, soups, fish, spinach, carrots, cheese and egg dishes and pumpkin pie.	Mace.
Oregano	A strong, pungent flavoured herb used mainly in Italian and Spanish cookery. Oregano is wild marjoram.	Tomato sauces, dressing, eggs, lentils, veal, beef and fish dishes.	Marjoram.
Paprika	Made from dried and ground ripe capsicums, paprika has a mild, slightly sweet flavour.	Hungarian Goulash, chicken, eggs, cheese, crab, potatoes and garnish for insipid food.	Small amount of cayenne pepper.
Parsley	The most versatile herb. It should be eaten raw, and is so unassertive that it complements most other herbs.	Nearly all savoury dishes and as a garnish.	
Rosemary	The needle-like leaves have a strong flavour and should be used discreetly.	Tomato dishes, lamb, veal, pork, stuffings, soup and in salad dressing.	Thyme.

	DESCRIPTION	USE	ALTERNATIVE
Saffron	An expensive spice used in cooking to impart yellow colour and a subtle flavour. Use sparingly, either in stigma or powder form. Steep saffron in a little warm water before using.	Fish soups, rice dishes.	
Sage	A pleasantly bitter and powerful herb that can counteract the richness of certain foods. Use sparingly.	Stuffing, rissoles, veal, cheese savouries, meatloaf, casseroles, beans and omelettes.	
Tarragon	A herb with a tart flavour and spicy aroma. It is essential in Bearnaise sauce and steeped in vinegar is delicious for salad dressings.	Fish, mayonnaise, salads, poultry, veal, liver and kidneys.	
Thyme	Present in bouquet garni and mixed herbs, it is one of the great culinary herbs. The small grey-green leaves blend well with marjoram and bay leaf.	All meats, fish, soups, stuffing, sauces, eggs, cheese, vegetables and salads.	Rosemary.
Turmeric	Turmeric gives food a bright yellow colour with a sharp mustard-type flavour.	Pickling, egg and meat dishes, seafood and rice.	

Index